NINE LIVES SQUARED

How to Live Life to the Nth Degree

JANE KING

Nine Lives Squared
© 2014 by Jane King

All rights reserved.

Printed in the United States of America.

No part of this book may be used or reproduced in any manner whatsoever without written permission except in the case of brief quotations embodied in critical articles and reviews. For information, address Caboodle Publishing at P.O. Box 460303, Aurora, CO 80046-0303.

This publication is designed to provide information in regard to the subject matter covered. In so doing, neither the publisher nor the author is engaged in rendering legal, accounting or other professional services. If you require legal advice or other expert assistance, you should seek the services of a professional specializing in the particular discipline required.

While the author has made every effort to provide accurate information at the time of publication, neither the publisher nor the author assumes any responsibility for errors, or for changes that occur after publication.

Caboodle Publishing books may be purchased for educational, business or sales promotional use. For information, please write:

Special Promotions Department, Caboodle Publishing, P.O. Box 460303, Aurora, CO 80046-0303.

First Edition

Published by Caboodle Publishing, Denver, CO.
Cover design – Caboodle Marketing, Inc.
ISBN: 978-0-9788799-9-0
ISBN-10: 0-9788799-9-6

INTRODUCTION

Once upon a time a caring and thoughtful guy had a lot of bad things happen to throughout his life and he chose to let it fester instead of dealing with it. He is truly a good guy that has always stopped to help others and doesn't turn away from someone in need. He is a hard worker and has always chosen physical labor jobs as that's what he loves. In fact, I have seen him work 36-hours straight with merely a cat nap.

The man I speak of is my brother Jim and the inspiration for this book. He is not a complainer and instead embraces what happens in his life by the way he thinks and what he believes. As you will see, he is living the universal laws and doesn't even know it. Unfortunately, in the wrong way.

For example, from a young child he was so angry, loud and obnoxious that I didn't want to be around him. I minimized my conversations with him and certainly didn't go out of my way to visit him. It was more than I could handle.

Then after his heart attack, bypass surgery and stroke, Jim changed completely. He realized that life is more precious than he ever thought. He was more loving, caring and actually there to help me. In fact, I lived with him and his wife in the winter months after my husband passed away. It's like it took this massive stroke to wake him up. He was forced to learn how to do everything again from using his fingers to tying his shoes. He was forced to put his mind power to good use and his physical rehabilitation, whereas in the past he let his mind only focus on the negative and the bad.

It has been amazing to see his progress. For example, when he was a child he was left-handed. Our father tied his left hand behind his back to make him learn to use his right hand. Now, he has learned to use both hands himself. It was his subconscious that kicked in and helped direct and guide him with the ingrained memory of what he is capable of and how he has spent his life.

He is also extremely sensitive and more open to new ideas, new techniques and new ways of being. When I started on my quest to expand my mind, I studied John Kehoe extensively. As Jim saw the results of what I was experiencing and how I was feeling, he took notice. He wanted to know more about the program and had a sincere desire to understand what it was all about.

Because Jim has lived in such a negative mental environment all of his life it has been a challenge for him to shift and embrace a more positive way of being. However, I give him credit because he is willing to try and that is more than can be said for a lot of people in the world. I even copied a series of John Kehoe mind power CD's that provides positive meditations for him.

He would sit by the wood stove in his garage, listening to the affirmations so he can anchor the positive thoughts into his subconscious. This has been powerful for him because I have seen a significant shift in how he interacts with all the people in his life. He is also working on forgiving our father as he has been holding anger from the time he was young. I guess someone on the outside may understand, however, I know that forgiving and moving on is critical and key.

After our father left suddenly our mother was not in a position to support all seven of us. So in order to "scrimp and save" Mom replaced real milk with powdered milk, which was far less expensive for such a large family. She bought the cheapest cuts of meat. Family and friends provided all the fruit and vegetables. We mostly wore hand-me-downs and slept 3 to a room. This environment impacted each of us kids from the way we acted to the people we married and how we conducted our adult lives.

Jim was constantly angry and was a magnet for bad luck and all that was bad in life as I share in this book. Me, I was different. I was extremely reserved and somewhat unconfident. I was failing in school and although my mother was an exceptionally strong woman and a mother of 7, she was home constantly working to try to make ends meet. Growing up, I could see she didn't want to fight with me about doing my homework or chores as she had already been through this with my 6 siblings. Mom and I locked horns often as she struggled through menopause, the same time I started puberty. I got married right out of school to a man that continued to make me feel weak. I felt subdued, inadequate and unintelligent. We pinched every penny we made. My husband kept telling me it was going to make us millionaires, and there was really a light at the end of the tunnel. We didn't even eat out EVER, and I mean EVER. We rarely took a vacation in all twenty five years of our marriage. All we did was work, come home, eat and then go to work again the next day. We did not have any hobbies or outside activities. In fact, our family would invite us out to eat and we would only order water and always pick the cheapest dish.

As I look back on it, I can see how people thought it was a bit crazy, but I lived it day in and day out so it was normal to me. My husband was a drinker though, and my family would tell me the conditions I was living in were not healthy or right. Yet, I didn't know any better.

It was normal to me because I was never on my own or exposed to any other way of being.

In fact, my husband was diagnosed with cancer at the age of 4 and lost his right arm. He overheard the doctors tell his mother he could die any time before he was 18. His mom always made sure she put a great meal on the table for him. However, when he moved out he was extremely frugal with his money and only bought the cheapest foods. He was now not only drinking, but maintaining a poor diet and was constantly on medication for arthritis and nervousness.

I worked every day and would simply hand over my paychecks to him. I recall one time when I felt pushed to my wits end. I stood up to him and refused to work 7 days a week. I started working only 5 days a week and I began to hate him. I resented the fact that he had pushed me to my limits and stifled me for all these years. I was out of my mind with anger and stress. I hated him, yet deep in my heart I loved him. I lived with this massive split of emotion for years. And in looking back, I know it contributed to my health, stress and physical feelings.

Then the time came. He was in his forties and he suffered massive brain damage. He lay in the hospital for 3 months in a coma before he finally passed away. I remember having this sick feeling inside because even though I knew I loved him, a part of me couldn't stand him and I felt completely lost. He had always taken care of everything and now I was left alone to do it all by myself. I had always been weak but decided that I would need to start somewhere.

I made a commitment to start taking care of myself. I began eating better, which included fruits & vegetables. I took money out of the bank to invest in personal development. I did the entire series of Peak Potentials courses, including Warrior and Wizard. Not an easy adventure for a meek, mild and weak woman. Yet, I did it. I was extremely proud of myself. I was starting to feel alive. I can't say I felt alive again because I'm not sure I have ever felt alive in all my life.

It was a strange, yet exciting and exhilarating feeling and I remember the key turning point for me. I was sitting in the audience at a John Kehoe event with a friend of mine and I said, "I'm going to do this!" He resonated with me. His message was motivating, inspiring and felt aligned with me. I started the course in 2011 and made massive changes. Jim saw the changes in me, and it was an inspiration to him as well.

But for me, I can feel myself changing. Prior to these programs I would seriously doubt that I could handle life on my own, let alone the hundreds of thousands we had and yes, we did end up being just shy of a million when my husband passed. With all of the work I was doing on myself I finally felt that I could handle anything that I was faced with. I would normally have a "man around" to fix things for me, yet I started to feel empowered to figure it out for myself.

I began to know without a doubt that the perfect answers and solutions exist right now inside of me. I never felt that certain about anything in all of my life. I started to pay attention to what I knew. I started to spend time on what I love to and started to spend money, energy and time doing the things that I truly enjoy.

The more I do, the happier and more fulfilled I feel. I also started to see how many opportunities were coming my way. I started to have amazing things happen in my life. I began to trust what I felt and believed that I was attracting the life that I not only wanted, but rather deserved. I am truly grateful every day of my life now. I have forgiven my husband as I now realize that I wouldn't be morphing into the person I am without having those experiences, and I would not have had my financial resources without my years with him.

I have come a long way, but the one thing that I am now working on is feeling pretty. I realize that I now need to make the outside match the inside. I never had anyone tell me that I am pretty and

I certainly never felt pretty. Until now that is. I am eating right, exercising, taking vitamins and it shows. I have a healthy glow about me. When I was married I never exercised, I only worked. Now I take time every day to nurture and pamper myself.

I am also starting to dress differently. As I see it, it is more aligned with who I have become. I am buying colors that I would have never purchased before, yet when I wear them I feel even more empowered than ever before. I am even proud that my son has shed 20 pounds. It makes me feel like I am finally being a good role model for him and that as a young adult, I am helping to set him up for a life of success and empowerment.

What I have realized in this entire process is that anyone can do anything they put their mind to, and I am living proof. If I can transform my life to what I have now in less than 3 years, then anyone can shift and create lasting change. I have such a strong passion and desire to help people understand that no matter what their upbringing, background or history, you can achieve anything.

You can truly make your mind think anything you want it to. In fact, your mind is not in charge of you, *you are in charge of your mind.* Before I embarked on my life transformation process I would just go along with anything that my mind was saying. I would let my mind run away and I would tend to ramble. I have been embarrassed in the past with this, but now have learned that I am in control of my mind.

I view myself as having always been a "regular" person just going along with life. I would spend my days in a rut not taking note of those around me and I was never "present" to situations or experiences. I can't say that I was grateful; I was more resentful. I was not honoring myself and I certainly did not know of or appreciate the universal laws.

In looking at everything that happened to my brother throughout his life and the transformation I have brought about in my life, I decided to write this book. A book to inspire, motivate and relate to every "regular" person out there. Every person that may deep down inside have a glimmering thought that there is more to life but have an uncertainty of what to do and how to achieve it.

It is simple and most of all, it's FREE. Your mind is free and training your mind is free. It just takes commitment, discipline and guidance. I'm going to share with you all of Jim's stories, and then tie in the universal laws so you can begin to have a greater understanding.

Sit back, relax and enjoy the stories. Then at the end I will share some affirmations and offer some guidance so that you may begin the adventure of transformation. Congratulations for being open to explore this opportunity, and committing to expanding your understanding.

CHAPTER 1
Intuition - Your Animal Instinct

Intuition - *The act or faculty of knowing or sensing without the use of rational processes; immediate cognition.*

It is often said that intuition is the most attuned gift a person can possess. However, I believe that it is only the most attuned gift if a person recognizes it, appreciates it, fosters it and listens to it. The gut is actually a mass of neural tissue that is filled with neurotransmitters and it handles a lot more than merely the digestion of food. Many refer to the gut as the "second brain" because it consists of sheaths of neurons that are embedded in the walls of the gut. In fact, this so-called second brain contains over 100 million neurons, which is more than your spinal cord or your peripheral nervous system.

Scientists have found that about 90% of the fibers in the gut carry information to the brain, not the other way around. A large part of your emotions are triggered by the feelings in your gut. It is interesting that the term "gut feeling" does not actually originate in the gut. It has been proven that it originates in the subconscious mind, which sends a message through the nervous system to the gut.

The role of the conscious mind is to interpret the meaning behind these feelings, thus making it a complete cycle in the body. When the subconscious mind receives information, it relates it almost instantaneously with past experiences, images and feelings. This is the trigger for good, bad or neutral feelings in the gut.

Many times in my life I have been tuned into my gut feelings and have honed it even more as I have gone through life. Lately, after Jeff passed, I have tried to make every decision based on my gut feeling. However, my brother is the opposite. In fact, I'm not sure he even knows what a gut feeling is. I think most of the time he believes it is a feeling of hunger or indigestion. I have tried to explain to him the importance of being in tune. However, he just didn't hear it.

There are several instances that I recall where he could have shifted the outcome if he had been aligned with his intuition. Let me share a few of them with you.

A few years ago on a beautiful fall day my brother Jim asked me to go for a ride with him. I agreed and we hopped on his ATV and we headed down a winding dirt road. The scenery was gorgeous. The trees had just started to turn, the air was crisp and there was a woodsy scent that reminded me of chopping wood as a child. I was gazing around and enjoying the view when my brother abruptly stopped the ATV in the middle of the road. As I looked forward I saw two deer standing in front of us. They were staring straight at us. I got off the ATV and walked to the side of the road. My gut instinct told me to move out of the way and admire from the distance. Jim stayed on the ATV with the engine running. In fact, he revved it slightly to see if the deer in front of him would move. They didn't move, but a few seconds later a deer came charging out of the ditch running straight for Jim. The deer got right next to the ATV and all of a sudden leaped in the air. Jim looked up to see the deer just as the deer's hoof clobbered him on the head. The deer hit him so hard that it knocked him off the ATV completely. I went running over to him and he was dazed and confused. As he started to raise his head, I could see the dent on his helmet. Thank goodness he decided to wear one. He normally never wears a helmet, but luckily he did that day. He would have been seriously injured without his helmet.

A few days later, we were all sitting around the dinner table discussing the incident. I kept wondering why he didn't get off the ATV, and furthermore why he revved the engine. My intuition clearly told me to get off and move to the side and I would have guessed that revving the engine could agitate the deer and cause it to charge towards us.

Jim said that he felt a tingling in his stomach and another feeling, but he thought he was just hungry and maybe a bit nervous being that close to two deer. He didn't think anything of that feeling, and in his mind he revved the engine because he wanted to see how tame the deer were. If they would run then he would know they were not accustomed to being around people and ATV's.

I tried to explain that the feelings in his stomach was his intuition trying to warn him and protect him. Yet, he just didn't get it. He said he didn't know how to interpret that meaning.

Jim's family was in Florida watching a golf tournament and all of a sudden there was an overwhelming gasp that waved through the crowd. As they turned to their right and looked, they could see people pointing toward the water near the ninth hole. That was the water hole right next to them. They saw two animal control specialists sprint onto the green. One had an electrical prod in his hand and the other had a long metal stick with a harness at the end of it. As one was prodding, the other was moving towards the head to loop the harness around the gator. They stood in amazement and watched. The guy got the noose around the gator's head and just as the crowd was ready to breathe a sigh of relief, the gator swished violently and broke loose of the noose.

People were screaming, panicking and started to run away. Jim's family ran with the crowd yet Jim ran in the opposite direction. It's like he had a mind of his own. He was running in the wide open grassy area and everyone else was running into the trees where the wooded area was dense with coverage. It would have been difficult for an alligator to maneuver into the wooded area so instinctively so that's where the crowd ran. Not Jim. As Jim was running he turned to look and it was as if the gator locked eyes with him. Jim paused for a moment and then the game was on. The gator snapped and growled loudly and took off after Jim. It was as if the gator had a massive burst of speed. The animal control men were sprinting after the gator trying to catch up.

They finally did catch up and used the electrical prod to slow the gator's speed. That allowed the other guy to get near the gator's head and put the noose back on. Jim kept running and didn't stop until he got to the club house. His family had never seen him run so fast in their lives.

When everyone sat down for a drink that night, Jim was asked why he ran in the opposite direction. He said he thought it would be the fastest way out. Curious, someone asked why he didn't follow the crowd and trust in their instinct. He simply said he had never followed a crowd in his life and wasn't about to start.

It wasn't even about following the crowd. He could have gotten seriously injured because his conscious mind took over the instinct in his gut. The fight or flight that gives you direction and guidance had been overridden. It was the flight mode, but the GPS had been turned off! They tried to prove their point by telling him that everyone else had followed their instinct that told them to move to safety, and that safety was not speed and rather finding cover. His mind told him to direct the gator away from his family, which in turn endangered his life further.

I have to say that thinking back it would have been rather hilarious to see the gator chasing my brother down the fairway on the golf course.

On Jim's next trip to Florida they decided to go water boating. He figured it would be safe since they would be in a boat and he would not have a chance to get chased by an alligator. They drove up to this backwoods place that had so much character. The way they described it, I think the shack could have been in a movie. It had old metal Coca Cola™ signs hammered on the outside with rusty edges, the wood plank siding looked like it came off of a hundred-year-old barn, and the windows had that hazing coverage around the corners leaving only a small hole to see through in the middle. He smiled as they got out of the car because he knew this was going to be a fun adventure.

As they walked through the rickety doorway they spotted a man in bib overalls. No shirt, just bib overalls and shoes that must have been ten years old. He had a twangy drawl to his voice, and Jim had a gut feeling that this was going to be a good trip on the water because he certainly wasn't a transplant. He was clearly a native.

He directed us out back and as we were walking down the pathway Jim started gawking at how the moss and kudzu was growing in the trees. He kept looking up and walking. He was clearly off the path. The people there turned around just in time to watch him step on an alligator. Yes, he stepped right on the gator and kept right on walking. He didn't skip a beat. The gator raised its head, snapped and growled, but did not go after Jim.

Someone screamed and the guide stopped dead in his tracks. They hollered at Jim and he finally became aware of what had just happened. Someone asked him what in the heck he was doing not paying attention. He simply said that he got caught up looking at the kudzu and thought he simply stepped on a log.

I couldn't believe that he didn't have a clue that he had wondered so far off the path, and that his gut didn't signal loudly that he was

15

approaching danger. Well, I guess I shouldn't say that I can't believe it. I know that his gut signaled him; he just ignored it as usual.

He is just lucky that the alligator was not hungry as he would have enjoyed Jumbo Steak for dinner!

As a kid, I remember going to the Algonquin Park where we would go camping. This was primitive camping, with us sleeping in tents and sleeping bags, cooking over the campfire and having to use an outhouse for the "facilities." Yet, it was fun times. We were together as a family and we were out in the fresh air in the woods. At this particular time it was fall and my parents wanted to take us one last time before the cold set in.

We had spent the first night around the campfire. My mother made a delicious dinner and we all told jokes and laughed until our stomachs hurt. I certainly slept soundly that night because I was plum worn out. I woke up to Jim huffing and puffing so loudly I thought there was a bear in our campground.

He was so loud it woke up Mom and she came racing out of their tent. It wasn't a bear and rather it was Jim standing next to the fire pit, hunched over gasping for air. Mom asked him what happened and he said that he had gone to the outhouse to go to the bathroom and as he came out, he wasn't paying attention and tripped over a bear.

The bear growled and Jim screamed at the top of his lungs. It scared Jim half to death and must have scared the bear as well because the bear ran in the opposite direction of Jim. Jim had sprinted all the way back to camp and could hardly tell the story.

I asked him years later if he sensed anything as he walked out the door and he explained that he wasn't even thinking or paying attention. Amazing to me that the bear didn't attack him.

I remember stories about growing up on the farm. We had all kinds of animals and the one prize possession of my father's was an 800 pound pig. Yes, it weighed 800 pounds… my father weighed it on the farm. As kids, we knew better than to mess with the pig because it was so large. Dad always told us how dangerous it could be for us to be around the pig. We were forbidden from the pig pen.

Let's just say that didn't stop my mischievous brother Jim. He had seen how our father used a squirt bottle to get the pig to mind. Dad used that trick whenever the pig got out and he wanted to corral him back into the pen. One day, Jim got the bright idea to jump in the pen and use the water bottle to practice training the pig. He thought that if he did that, the next time the pig got out he could prove to our father how "big" he was by helping to get the pig back in the pen.

He stared the pig in the eyes and then squirted the pig right on the nose. That is the worst place to squirt a pig. Dad always squirted on the face but never right square on the nose. That pig took off after Jim and rammed him square in the stomach. He was thrown against the fence and as he hit the ground the pig rooted him again with his snout and throw him up on the air like a rag doll.

I remember hearing Jim scream for help and we all ran to the pen. When we got there, Jim had managed to crawl under the fence and was just outside the pen. He had a bloody nose, swollen eye and was doubled over. Mom nursed him back to health but he had quite a shiner for over a week.

I asked him why he squirted the pig in the nose, and Jim said he thought it would get the pig's attention and be the best way to make him mind. I was curious and asked Jim if he sensed anything when he looked the pig in the eyes. He said he didn't feel anything, just thought the pig could see that he meant business, which would help him mind better.

Jim and dogs is a whole other string of stories. He has been attacked several times, bitten numerous times and had his clothes torn off and even once fought off a dog with his walker. To this day, I can't figure out why he hasn't taken the signals that have clearly been given

17

to him in his gut and learned how to trust his intuition.

I find it interesting that Jim has skated death by a deer, an alligator, a bear, a pig and several dogs. I look at all of the instances and understand that the universe has been trying to send a message to my brother Jim for nearly 60 years. Why can't he wake up and smell the toast? For goodness sake, it is burning!

I know that his conscious mind is overriding the signals that are being sent to his gut. They call this logic over instinct. It means that the brain is rationalizing what should be done and what steps should be taken rather than trusting the signal from the gut. The signal in its purest form is the message of guidance. But rationale and logic can override and outthink the best signal.

I wonder… how many other people in this world are unaware of the power of instinct and trusting their gut? I have honed my skills over the years and continue to do so today. I read books, journal and study daily. I listen to my body and spend time being still every day. I believe these practices are what has helped me be in tune and avoid any major accident or incident in my life.

CHAPTER 2
Attention - Rev Your Engine and Your Awareness

Attention - *Notice taken of someone or something; the regarding of someone or something as interesting or important.*

Attention is an interesting word, and actually ultimately defines us at a neurological level. What you place your attention on and for how long determines your programming. Attention even makes real things that were not real before. That's why people that place attention on their internal pain tend to have more internal pain. I'm not saying that you can "think" your pain away, but research has proven what you focus your attention on actually is enhanced.

If you are a negative person and focus on the worst case scenario, then you are programming negativity into your brain. You will start to see things even worse than they may actually be because of the attention you have placed on negativity. We all know pessimistic people. In fact, my brother Jim lived his entire life in this state. Always looking at the downside and continuing to tell himself every single day that he is just lucky to be alive is still a negative thought that is recurring instead of celebrating life. Bad things just naturally happen to him. In order for Jim to make a change, he has to personally want to. For most people, it takes one act or one incident to force them into shifting. This one act typically causes an extreme amount of pain or makes the person extremely uncomfortable. This level of discomfort is what drives the willingness to change and shift attention.

The beauty is that we have the ability to change the wiring in our brains. We can change our mind and literally change our brain. This is because the brain possesses such elasticity that it has the ability to shut down old pathways of thought and form new ones at any time. We have all heard the phrase, "Mind Over Matter." This is how it applies. You literally make a choice to shift your attention and change your mind.

For my brother Jim, he spent his entire life with his attention focused and never made time to just "be" in the moment enjoying nature, listening to the birds or watching clouds float by in the sky. After each incident happened, he would chalk it up to another bad thing that happened but didn't kill him. Even though most people would have been dead after just one event, let alone all of his mishaps.

We all drive our attention and our ability to live the life we chose. It's like a car. I believe that Jim has the ability to drive his destiny, yet with his car experiences he was being given signs and signals for over 40 years to make a shift. Shift gears and change his life… Yet he continued to ignore these signs and therefore continued to place his attention on the negative. He never allowed his body to be re-energized with positivity and to just clear his mind.

Just read what happened to him in a car. Can you say that you would have taken the hint after the first three incidents? Most would have after the first, let alone all of these. It is serious, yet it makes me chuckle. I always thought he was just hard-headed and now I realize that he just doesn't know what he doesn't know. I wondered how many others are out there in the world in the same situation. That's why I am so passionate about telling Jim's story and sharing with you all that has happened because if he can overcome several heart attacks, strokes and thrive, so can you… No matter what your circumstances are.

It was the year of the Corvette, 1963. A time when my brothers were free in spirit and wild in every way. Bob wanted to show off his bright red Corvette and let them see how fast it would go. Lance was the co-pilot with Jim in the back seat. Bob punched the gas and squealed the tires and sped into the night. They were on the 401 highway, and Bob had the peddle to the metal. In a matter of no time at all they were doing 140 mph. Lance make the mistake of not asking Bob if he had ever driven a car at that speed before. For any of you that have, you know that every car reaches a speed where almost appears to take on a life of its own. It feels as if the car is floating and you have no control.

That was at 140 mph for this car and Bob quickly realized that he was in over his head. He lost control of the car and it hit the shoulder and they went airborne. Lance and Bob were thrown from the car, which saved them as they landed on the soft dirt in the ditch. Jim on the other hand, was trapped in the back seat. In the Corvette, the back seat is virtually non-existent. Jim was wedged between the front seat and the back seat. Thank goodness he was. Otherwise, he would have merely rolled around in the car like a rag doll as it flipped several times. He hit the consol and was knocked unconscious. Paramedics believe that is what saved him as it allowed his body to go completely limp and he wedged perfectly in a safe spot.

Jim was lucky, yes. I look at this situation and believe that his subconscious took over to ensure he was safely tucked in a spot to avoid injury. His attention was not in the right place at the time as he was acting wild and crazy, and the bottom line here is that he is not the nicest person. Was this a sign from the universe for him to drive his life in a new direction? To wake up and take notice? To place his attention on the things that matter most in life? If it was, Jim didn't listen.

A couple of years later, Jim was out with his friends and it was the wee hours of the morning. There were four people in the car and Jim was in the passenger seat next to the door. Something jolted him, and thank goodness! Everyone in the car had fallen asleep, including the driver. Jim bolted up in the seat, yelled and hit the driver's shoulder. Startled he awoke and realized they were headed for a train. His buddy swerved the car and they hit the side of the train. They were dragged over 1,000 feet. The car finally broke loose and ended up in a wooded area. Their buddy that was riding in the middle of the front seat clawed Jim severely trying to get out to the car. The claw marks were so deep there were piles of skin at the base of each claw mark. None of the other passengers were injured, just Jim. He spent hours in the hospital getting treatment for his bruises since it was his side of the car that hit the train.

Was it the horn of the train that startled Jim? A signal from above to grab his attention? To this day no one knows. I have my beliefs, yet Jim just believes he is lucky. Avoided yet another close brush with death.

It was a beautiful summer day and Jim had been out the night before. He was exhausted but trying to function. He got in his car and realized his tire was almost flat. He pulled into the local station and asked if he could air for the tire. The mechanic on duty agreed and Jim pulled up to the door of the bay. He grabbed the hose, unscrewed the valve cap and began to air it up. He was so tired that he leaned over the tire and was using it to hold himself up. All of a sudden, there was a tremendous boom. The tire had blown, the rim (a flawed and split rim) had exploded and Jim was thrown nearly 100 feet into a Pontiac car parked in the lot. As he melted down the side door of the Pontiac, Jim had blood gushing everywhere. Turns out a piece of the rim had hit his forehead just above his left eye and another chard gashed his leg just below the knee cap. He did several hundred dollars worth of damage to the Pontiac he hit, too. The paramedics told him that if he had been upright just six inches from the tire, he would have taken the entire brunt of the impact in his chest and would have been killed. But, because he was leaning on the tire, he was thrown back by the blast. Six inches was the difference between living and dying that day.

You may be thinking that because he was not paying attention, his life was spared. That could be the case or it may be that if he had been paying attention to the air going into the tire, it would not have reach a point where it exploded. We can pay attention to the smallest of details and many of them can have the most profound impact on our lives. Paying attention to the smallest detail of the pressure of the tire and the valve could have prevented it all. No one can second guess incidents that happen. I just know that paying attention is critical in life.

Jim loves cars, always has. He was in an amateur race in our local town and he was doing well. They were on the last lap and as he crossed the line, he saw the checkered flag wave in front of the car. I watched from the stands and wasn't worried because Jim was in a car that had a 5-point safety harness, he was wearing a helmet with a face shield, had armor plate glass for a windshield, a roll cage and several other safety features. All of a sudden, a car in front of Jim spun out of control and ended up hitting Jim head on. One would think Jim was safely tucked in his car and would avoid injury. Not the case. The impact of the two cars caused the fan blade to come flying out of the other car and it came in the side window at an angle that would be nearly impossible to re-create. It hit Jim directly in the throat. He was in the hospital for days, and even now he still has difficulty talking sometimes and can hardly have a tube placed down his throat.

He had paid attention and had all of his safety gear in place.

However, I wonder if some higher power was trying to get his attention in life. Wanting him to shift his ways and become a happier and better person.

It was a nice evening and Jim was driving home. He was going the speed limit and minding his own business. All of a sudden, he saw a car swerving at him head on. The car was clearly out of control and speeding. It was going 60 mph in a 40 mph zone. Jim was not wearing a seat belt and the head on impact threw Jim into the windshield. His head was buried in the glass including his eyebrows. Just as that impact occurred, Jim was hit from behind by a car going nearly 40 mph and that jolted Jim's head backwards out of the windshield. It tore the skin and he was left sitting in the seat a bloody mess. He was rushed to the hospital and kept for several days. It took him over a month for all of the glass to surface that had been embedded underneath his skin. Police later told Jim they thought the driver of the car was having a heart attack, which is why he sped up and lost control. I believe this is the law of attraction, and for some reason Jim is attracting these things.

He thought he was paying attention to the road and minding his own business. Yet again, slowing your thoughts and thinking of noting lets your mind rejuvenate. I believe someone was trying to gain his attention and awaken him to his potential and help him realize all that he could be in this world.

Jim was driving to work one day. Enjoying the scenery and going the speed limit. He was admiring the river and noticing how it was flowing nicely. Thinking it was nice instead of some of the years past when the river was low. He saw a red flash in the corner of his eye and quickly looked in his rear view mirror. He looked up just in time to see a car start to go around him, but the car was too close. It was clearly going to hit Jim so he swerved and went over the edge. The car was airborne and landed front first in the water. Jim was banged up, but conscious. The river was shallow enough that the water only rose above his knees. When the ambulance arrived, he was still stunned and dazed in the car. They carefully got him out and loaded him up to take him to the hospital. On the way there, the ambulance was hit by a truck that ran a stop sign. The truck was going full speed just as the ambulance. The impact caused the ambulance to flip twice. It landed on its side. Jim was still strapped into the gurney, but he had been banged up as he hit the roof and sides of the ambulance. Another ambulance arrived quickly and they loaded Jim up. That ambulance sped away and on the way to the hospital, it was hit by a car. The ambulance didn't flip, but people were banged up. Jim, disgusted with all of his bad luck, demanded to be released as he was not going to get in another ambulance that day. He walked home and had the paramedics come to the house to treat him.

Many times we are reliant on others to be paying attention. The drivers of all vehicles, emergency or not, must be attentive. The attention level of several people was clearly low that day. Starting with the car that shoved my brother off the bridge. How can you be a vessel to help others become more aware and place more attention on their surroundings? I believe the law of attraction was working that day. The other people that were out driving the other cars were all attracting accidents, especially since it was one right after the other.

I remember when Jim decided to go to Leamington. It was a long drive and he set out to drive it in one hour. I wouldn't have done it in one hour, but many people had. Jim left early in the morning and was driving when he saw this white flash coming towards the windshield. As he kept driving, he got closer and realized it was a bird. Typically birds fly near the windshield and then dive away. Not this bird. The seagull was not fast enough to avoid the windshield. It hit so hard that it came through the windshield and was in the passenger seat flailing and flapping its wings. Annoyed, he drove slowly with the hazard lights flashing until he reached a gas station. He called his boss, "Marty" who sent a tow truck, towing a car for Jim to drive the rest of the way. Jim got in the second car and drove about a half hour, then KABOOM. Out of nowhere, he was hit by a car. Jim was fine but just shook up. This car was no longer fit to drive so Jim asked the police to call his boss who sent out a third car and took the wrecked one back to the shop again. On the road again and closer to Leamington, a farmer with an overloaded hay wagon coming out from his field, didn't see Jim coming and hit his car right in the driver's side door. Luckily, the farmer had stopped and just started to accelerate. The damage to the door was extensive so another tow truck was called and he was on his way again in his bosses wife's new Monte Carlo. As the car climbed a hill, he headed into an area of icy road. Jim grasped the wheel with both hands, and felt relieved as he saw it was a state sanding truck in front of him. "That actually wasn't a saving grace". The state truck slid sideways as Jim was coming around him. Jim swerved and went over the edge. The car plunged into a ditch with nearly 4 feet of water in it. His car was tightly wedged into the mud at the bottom of the ditch and he hit with such force that the car doors would not open and Jim could not break the windshield. The car started to fill with water and Jim was stuck. He found a small air pocket by the gas pedal. He gasped and inhaled, panicking, thinking that this was it. Emergency crews arrived and got him out of the car. He was in the hospital overnight for observation.

Needless to say, he never made it to Leamington that day. When you become so attuned, aware and are paying attention, you will recognize the road signs as they appear. I pay attention to all of my surroundings and after the first incident, I would have realized that I was not to be in Leamington that day. But Jim is not that attuned so he wasn't paying attention to the signs. He kept plowing forward and finding new ways and avenues to get there. Until the final one put him in such a spot that he could not continue on the journey. Pay attention to the road signs around you as they will guide you and serve you well. Don't ignore them as this will only cause the signals to get stronger and have a greater negative impact on you.

Our family was always playing pranks on one another. Most of them were harmless and funny. Pierre, our brother-in-law, decided to play a prank on Jim. Jim was driving a large dump truck up a massive pile of dirt on a construction site. Pierre told Jim to turn right after rock #23. Pierre did so knowing that it was to have been blocked off the day before. Pierre stood at the bottom watching Jim drive up, laughing inside. Thinking about how shocked Jim will be when he turns right and it's blocked off. Well, Pierre didn't know that the crew missed the deadline the day before. Jim carefully counted rocks and at #23, he turned right. Went over the edge of the pile and onto the neck of a crane. The dump truck slid all the way down the neck of the crane and smashed into the cab. Jim luckily was not hurt, but he was kept in the hospital overnight for his nerves.

Pierre hadn't paid attention to the crew's work. He didn't realize it wasn't blocked off. In life, each of us needs to be aware of all aspects of our surroundings. We need to understand the potential impact our level of attention has on others. Pierre didn't play a prank on my brother Jim again. He learned his lesson and was more vigilant with details on the job site after that.

A few years later, Jim was driving a tow truck. We had just had a wet spring snow storm so the roads were slushy, but not icy. It was the end of a long day and Jim was ready to go home. He had picked up a car from an accident scene and was ready to call it a day. It was pitch black and he was exhausted. He went under Ambassador Bridge. As a plow was clearing the bridge it started to throw down chunks of slushy icy snow onto Jim's windshield. Jim hit the gas in order to regain visibility, as he did so he veered left hitting a tree head on. The car he was towing slammed through the cab of the truck pinning Jim in the driver's seat. The plow, so far above and well past him by now, didn't see the accident so Jim was there over night. The tree he hit was at the entrance of a graveyard and Jim was wedged in the front seat and couldn't move a thing. It was so dark that all he could see was the light from the CB radio, but he couldn't reach it. He finally got squeezed over enough where he could press the button on the microphone. He just shouted, "I don't know what happened, I don't know where I am, but I've been in an accident." He unknowingly spent the night in the graveyard that has 13 generations of his relatives, shivering and freezing in the trapped truck. It took them until the next morning to find him. They had to wait for daylight to break. Jim luckily only had surface wounds and had not lost a lot of blood through the night. He was taken to the hospital and treated for his wounds and hypothermia.

Was it a coincidence that Jim looked at the graveyard all night long? I don't think so. I believe it was a sign to grab his attention. A literal demonstration of what is possible if Jim did not take notice and pay close attention.

It was a time of turmoil and the teamsters in Detroit were on strike. Things were heating up and getting violent. Jim had dislocated his ribs and had been cooped up in the house for a few days. He was ready for a break. His buddy called and asked if Jim wanted to go for a ride in his flat bed truck as he made a delivery. Of course, Jim wanted to go. As they were driving under the overpass they heard three loud pops. Turns out the teamsters had shot three times into the passenger side of the truck. The passenger side of the delivery truck is usually unoccupied so these were clearly meant to be warning shots. Because of Jim's dislocated ribs, he was not able to sit up straight. He was leaning toward the dash of the truck. Thank goodness. One bullet zinged right by his head, one went through his coat between his chest and arm and one hit the head rest. All three bullets would have been deadly had Jim been sitting upright in the seat.

The teamsters were sending a "friendly" signal to get the attention of Jim's buddy. Yet, the attention grabbing gesture could have easily been lethal had Jim not been suffering from dislocated ribs. What was the real attention grabber? Should Jim and his buddy have been paying more attention to the route they were taking and their surroundings? Not sure, but I know that the universe will send warning signs and deliver them in various ways.

Jim's incidents are not just reserved for vehicles. He had two incidents on his riding lawnmower tractor. He had removed the grass cutting blades and used this as a way to putt around town to and from local businesses. After his heart attacks and strokes he thought this was a faster way to get around since he couldn't walk well. He road this like many would ride a golf cart. One day he was riding the mower and had his daughter's dogs on an extended leash. They were going slow and he was enjoying the fresh air. They came around a corner by Burger King and were starting to cross the street when a woman came out of the parking lot and punched the gas. As she did that, she clipped the dogs leash and dragged Jim's lawnmower and the dogs into the middle of the intersection. Cars were screeching to a halt everywhere. Luckily, no one hit Jim and the dogs were fine.

Just a few days later, Jim was leaving the chiropractor on his lawnmower. He was headed across the street in front of Burger King again when he was hit on the rear fender by a car. It spun Jim into the intersection yet again. He said he felt like it was déjà vu as he was whisked into the intersection and stopped at almost the same angle as the last time. Yet again, cars came to a screeching halt and Jim was not hurt, just shaken up.

One would think that he would stay off the lawn mower for a while and drive a car. But he couldn't since he had lost his driver's license after the strokes. He couldn't figure it out because the lawn mower was painted bright green and had two long orange flags waving from the backend. He felt that would have grabbed the attention of any car near him. Obviously, he was not as attention-grabbing as he thought. Are you going through life thinking that you are garnering the attention of others, when in fact no one is noticing you? Are you waving flags or just showing up as a bright, positive and energetic person? My brother was actually bright and energetic, but not positive in his life so I believe that he could have had twenty flags flying and people still would not have paid attention.

Another incident occurred when Jim was driving his boss' Monte Carlo. He was heading back to work after running an errand. He wasn't speeding, merely taking his time and driving leisurely. As he was driving he saw a blur coming towards him. He turned his head just in time to feel the impact of a woman who ran a stop sign. She creamed the passenger side of the car and spun Jim in front of an on-coming car. The driver of that car panicked and hit the gas pedal instead of the brake. By the time it was all said and done, this was a 5 car pileup with Jim in the middle of it all. I am just thankful that it was all low-impact so no injuries. Jim was just shaken up and bruised a bit from all of the impacts.

It is proven that the stronger a person's concentration is, the stronger the signals that are sent to the neurons in the brain. This then triggers a more rapid firing of neurons. The more attention you pay in life, the more stimulated your neurons are. This helps create a new circuitry, if you will, in the brain. Focused attention can literally reprogram how you think, feel and act.

I look at Jim and see a walking lesson for everyone to take notice of. He has lived way more than nine lives, yet is just now beginning to learn how to pay attention to the universe and the road signs. A friend of mine once told me, "Pay attention to the road signs and the road will pave itself in front of you." Jim has been given so many road signs in his life, yet has not known how to pay attention to them. It makes me wonder what more he could have done or been had he paid attention. Then I take comfort in believing that me sharing his stories will help millions of people around the world understand the importance of paying attention and embracing the universe and spirituality, while giving yourself and mind some down time. It's important to look at the nature that's all around you. Taste an apple and really feel the grass under your feet. I find it best to keep life simple and I always make time to smell the roses.

CHAPTER 3
Attraction – Talk to the Hand

Attraction - *The act or capability of attracting.*

The law of attraction became a household phrase primarily after the launch of the book *The Secret* and all of the subsequent products that followed. If you have not read this book, I recommend it. Basically, it describes the principle of attraction. You attract what you think. When you shift to a higher energy and resonate more within the harmony and intention of being positive and living positively, you attract more of this energy into your life. You have to focus on stopping your mind, taking down time and also slowing your thoughts, which will allow the spiritual side of life to take over and rule out any potential "hectic" activity in your normal life.

If you are living in a world filled with negativity and you choose to embrace negativity, live with negativity and believe negative thoughts, you will attract more drama and negative events. The universe as a force never complains. It creates and offers options for greatness. When you feel completely connected and in harmony with your intention and purpose on this earth, you will attract more of what you need in order to accomplish and achieve even more.

Remember that every action of giving creates an opposite action of receiving. What you receive is always equal to what you've given. When you give positive thoughts and feelings, you can change your entire life. When I am feeling joyful, I am giving joy to others and will continue to receive joy. When you feel good, life will be good.

So often people have reactions to the things that happen around them. They have their feelings tied to the reactions or responses of others. The phrase that I love is, "It's not what happens to you, but how you react that matters most." It starts by having a vision inside of what you want your life to look like on the outside. You will produce in your environment what you continually see in your mind. This is the law of attraction.

Many need a helping hand to see the way so they can be more open to believing and envisioning more for themselves and their lives. It is not a coincidence that my brother Jim had so many mishaps with his hands. I believe he is supposed to be lending a hand to help more people, but yet has he seen the light and the way to do so.

Jim was a young man and was at work wearing his heat-resistant leather welding gear. He was a good welder and for those not familiar, being a welder is a skill and talent. Talented welders create master pieces with their work. He had on the hot asphalt gloves that went all the way up to his elbow. Jim's co-worker was not paying attention and moved a 700-degree blow torch over Jim's right glove, panicked and left it over Jim's left glove. It melted the glove to Jim's hand. Paramedics had to use tin snips to remove the glove because it was as solid as metal on Jim's hand and they were afraid they were cutting all of the skin. Jim's hand was bubbling burnt with near third-degree burns. His right hand had first-degree burns. He lost part of the webbing on his left hand and his thumb was burned black throughout. He spent nearly a week in the hospital and a few months recovering. I remember his talking about the pain and how angry he was with his co-worker.

Jim didn't intend for this to happen. But he was an angry person that fell into the trap of blaming others for mishaps and events. This was no exception. I wanted to explain to him the law of attraction and how kindness begets kindness. Yet, he was not in the space or frame of mind to be able to receive this message, let alone embrace it and move towards living a life with this belief.

A few years ago Jim was cleaning the chainsaw as he was getting ready for the winter season of cutting wood. He enjoys that every year, looking forward to being in nature with the smell of the woods. The chain he was cleaning and sharpening tangled and twisted along with his fingers. He had to hold the chain tight with the mangled hand while he calmly used the other to stop the wheel and overheat the motor until it stalled. He was able to slowly release his fingers, when he did they were filled with dirt, grease and blood. Thank goodness his wife was home and able to drive him to the hospital. The emergency room was packed so he ended up sitting in a trauma room for over 10 hours waiting to be seen by a doctor. The doctor examined him and all ten fingers were mangled or cut. The doctor recommended amputating four fingers. My brother refused. He was able to keep all ten fingers, but to this day some areas are so delicate that the slightest bump will cause bleeding and splitting of the skin. Thankfully, today Jim still has 95% usage of his hands. I believe God was guiding him on that journey as most people would have passed out before they even got into a vehicle. He was determined to keep all of his fingers, and he did. I believe he had the will power to keep his hands intact because they were going to be used for a much greater purpose in his lifetime.

I remember once when Jim stopped alongside the road to help one of his friends. He had a flat tire and had gotten the car jacked up and was in the process of taking the tire off. His friend had long legs so it was next to impossible for him to sit with his legs crossed, so he did what was natural. He sprawled his legs underneath the car and was ready to take the tire off when Jim walked up. As Jim approached the car, his friend jolted the tire enough that the jack started to slip. Jim instinctively grabbed the metal bumper in an attempt to stop the car from falling and crushing his friend's legs. The old cars had metal bumpers with the sharp edge underneath. That's what Jim had grabbed and with such force that his finger got caught between the bumper and the jack. It cut off his middle finger between the nail and the first knuckle. His hand was trapped for over 10 minutes before help got there to lift the car off of the jack and release his hand. He ended up with forty five stitches in his middle finger and five stitches in the other finger.

Jim was spared his finger that day. I believe that God has great things in store for his hands and when he realizes his true internal power, it will be amazing. He was merely helping a friend in this situation, yet was not in a helping place of his life. This was not a normal act for him. Did he attract that injury? I'm not the one in control or in a position to say. What I do know is that he has powerful hands and when he decides to use them for a greater good it will be amazing.

Jim was working on a construction site. This job site involved working with concrete. They had rebar sticking up everywhere so every day when the guys arrived, it was like walking in a maze and mine field. It had rained and the cement was slick. Jim went to grab a tool and fell forward. He fell with such force that his left hand hit the 3" thick rebar and it poked completely through his left hand. He was able to grab a cement block to balance himself as blood went everywhere. Once he realized what had happened, he let out one hell of a loud yell. The guys on the job site came running and when they realized what had happened they were paralyzed with shock, until the foreman told one of the guys to go grab a blowtorch. They had to cut the rebar in order to free Jim and take him to the hospital. Amazingly, it missed all of the vital veins, muscles and tendons. He had stitches and got a terrible infection while trying to heal it. He also had to have five weeks of therapy to help him regain movement of his hand.

Many said he was lucky that he didn't have to have his hand amputated. I agree. I also know that his mindset was not in the most gracious space and he was not in a place of pure gratitude in his life. He was at a point where he would get up every day and wonder what was going to happen to him. When you wonder that, you attract incidents. That's just a fact on how it works.

It wasn't but a few months later that Jim was adding a basement under his St. Antoine home. He had several guys there helping him. As the guys were surveying the situation, they all agreed that one of the shoring posts had started to sink into the dirt. Jim decided to add a piece of steel to the shoring post to help support it. As he put the steel piece in place, the house shifted and dropped slightly. It pinned his left hand between the beam and the piece of steel. All of his friends came rushing over and tried to lift the house. Yes, they were literally lifting the house while some were prying, digging and trying all types of things to release his hand. The slow settling of the house kept him pinned. Finally, his friends were able to gain leverage underneath the beam. At least enough that they were able to raise the house enough to free his hand. It had pinched his thumb, index finger and part of his hand. It basically squashed his hand, but did not break the skin. He went to the hospital but there was nothing they could do since there weren't any bones broken or an open wound. It took Jim over three months to heal from the swelling and pain.

This is what I call raising the house. He attracted the right friends in his life that day who were able to muster the strength to literally raise the house off his hand. Had it been any other group of men, they may have stood around thinking and wondering what to do.

While waiting for paramedics and fire fighters to arrive, these guys were thrifty and smart. They knew what to do in order to release his hand and save it from significant damage. He certainly attracted the right people at the right time that day.

Jim has always had a love for cars. He tinkers with them and fusses with the engines. I think that he picked up a lot of his skills from our father, who was a mechanic. One day he was working on the carburetor of his car. He was holding the carburetor while using a large screwdriver to loosen the screws. The screwdriver slipped and went three quarters into his left hand. He had a delayed response to the pain then once it registered, he was screaming and bobbing his head up and down. We rushed him to the hospital where they spent time cleaning all of the grease and grime out of the wound. He luckily didn't need to have stitches.

He was rushing and used a screwdriver that was larger than what he needed. This meant he put more leverage on the top of the screw driver, which caused it to slip. I believe that if he had been more attuned, he would have been attracted to grab the right tool for the job. Many of you may not believe that, but when you live a life that is aligned, aware and fully in tune with your surroundings, this is what happens. Jim is not there yet, but you will see later in the book how he is making progress.

Jim got assigned to a job where he was working inside a sewer for the city. He had taken the manhole cover off and started going down the metal rung ladder. Part way down, he reached up to pull the manhole cover back onto the hole. He was having difficulty so he climbed up one more rung on the ladder, braced both legs and used both hands. With a jerking motion, the manhole cover slid quickly over the hole. So fast in fact that Jim couldn't get his hand out in time. The cover slid right on top of his hand. Yelling, his co-worker heard him and came running down the sewer pipe. He lifted the manhole cover and Jim told him to grab his lunch pail because it had ice in it. He packed his hand in the ice while his co-worker rushed him to the Leamington hospital. His hand was crushed and bleeding profusely. He had wrapped a shirt around it, but that wasn't doing much good. When they got to the emergency room he was rushed in and the doctor said he would need to amputate at the wrist. My brother refused. He asked them to repack the ice and had his co-worker drive him to the hospital in Windsor. When they got there, Jim learned that they wouldn't be able to provide the proper care for this type of injury. They repacked his hand in fresh ice and his co-worker drove him to Grace Hospital. When they got there, Jim was told that the doctor that could handle this type of injury was actually at Hotel Dieu Hospital. They packed him in new ice and rushed there. Once at that hospital, Jim had to wait over an hour to see the doctor. They rushed him into surgery and after a 15-hour operation they were able to restore the circulation. Jim had a 10-day stay in the hospital that time. He had to have a cast on his arm and it took nearly 4-months before he was somewhat back to normal. To this day he only has about 80% movement in that hand.

Jim didn't attract the right doctor the first time. He had to travel to several hospitals and then wait in order to get the doctor that could save his hand. It was a struggle for him and at that time, Jim was struggling in his life. I wonder if he had been attuned to the universe and dialed in, if he could have attracted the right doctor at the first hospital they drove to. I obviously can't say for certain, but I know in my life, now I'm able to attract the right people at the right time for what I need.

Jim was working on a special project. His company had won the bid to work on the steeple of the St. Alphonse Church. The company men had erected the scaffolding and had been on the job site for days. Jim was eating his lunch in the "safe zone" with his buddies. This is an area that is designated as the safe area on the work site. Not exposed to any potential harm. That was normally the case, but not for Jim. A co-worker was at the top of the scaffolding and the wind picked up. It knocked off his steel hard hat. It hit the scaffolding, bounced off the planks, hit a tree and bounced off a limb in such a way that it came flying towards Jim. Jim was resting his hand on a stack of concrete blocks while eating lunch and the hat's brim nailed the top of his hand. No one could have ever even planned this fluky scenario. Yet, for Jim it happened. He quickly lifted his hand and shoved it into his lunch pail. Thank goodness he always put an ice pack in his lunch box. They rushed him to the hospital where they had to use several needles and a drain tube to prevent the swelling and drain the fluid. It looked like a deflated balloon when he went back to work. He was forced to do a lot of desk duty and paperwork for months until his hand healed.

Why did the hat hit Jim in the hand? How did the hat hit him? For months, Jim and his co-workers re-hashed that day and were not certain they could ever re-create the scenario that would have caused the hat to hit his hand in that particular way at that particular time. The wind, scaffolding, planks and trees were all at the correct angle to cause this to happen. Many would say that the law of attraction was at work and because Jim was out of alignment, he was attracting misfortune in his life. Not sure, but I am living proof that the law of attraction works in both positive ways and negative ways.

On the work site yet again, Jim had another incident. He was working and a steel sliver nearly 5 inches in length and $1/16^{th}$ of an inch thick went into the palm of his hand and came out the other side near his index finger. This incident was the most painful for Jim. He was in therapy for nearly six months and still has limited mobility in his hand. And he can't figure out how it all happened because it was so quick. That's why I can't tell the story in any more detail, because we just don't know.

Isn't it interesting that the most painful incident is the one that Jim can't remember how it happened? He has no recollection of the details surrounding that accident, yet remembers the agonizing pain it caused at the time of the accident and then for months afterwards during his rehab. I find it interesting that this is the case and just wonder how it really happened.

Jim was on scaffolding at another job site when he was in the fortunate position to save another man's life. They were handing planks up from the bottom to the guys on the top. One guy handing to the next to the next and so on. Jim took the plank from the guy below him and handed it to the guy above him. It slipped out of the hands of the guy above him just as Jim looked up. He knew that the guy below him was bent over to grab the next plank and would never see this plank coming. Jim put his hands up to grab the plank and he got a large sliver in the meaty part of the webbing between his thumb and index finger. It really wasn't a sliver, it was more like a chunk because it was ¼ inch by ½ inch by 6 inches in length. That's the chunk that peeled off the board as he tried to grab it. His co-worker climbed the scaffolding to Jim and pulled out his cutters to finish getting the chunk off of the plank. He helped Jim down to safety where they were able to then cut off his glove and take him to the hospital. The first hospital they went to didn't have a specialist to handle this type of injury so they went to the next hospital. They removed the sliver and he had damage to his knuckle and tendon. He also had sprained both wrists and injured his shoulder from trying to brace himself on the scaffolding. He spent nearly a month in therapy and after nearly 30-years, he still has pain. He even has calcified wooden slivers that still surface and need to be removed by doctors.

Did his co-worker attract Jim as the one above him? I don't know, but I know that Jim was there for a reason and able to assist in saving this guy's life. The plank would have easily killed the guy below Jim.

Yet Jim didn't hesitate to raise his hands and attempt to grab a plank flying towards him. In fact, this was just one example of many where Jim saved others lives. I believe other people attracted Jim to actually save their life.

It has been said that a person's presence allows others to feel unified or disconnected. It all depends upon how the person shows up, chooses to live and be. The effect of being in the presence of people who express themselves in high frequencies is to feel unified and connected to all of nature, all of human kind and all with the right intention.

A person's presence can influence so many others and in a positive way when you come from a place of love, gratitude and appreciation. Jim has not fully discovered how to show up, be present and be in alignment with the universe. It is not easy to learn, and takes awareness and time. It takes commitment to study, learn and be willing to actively participate.

I do believe that he has been spared his hands in order to do even greater good in the world in the coming years. He may not know all that he is intended to do, but I have no doubt that when he steps into the right mindset, he will be afforded the opportunity to have a tremendous impact on those around him. I look forward to being part of that journey and a witness to that process.

CHAPTER 4
Impact - The power of your thoughts

Impact - *The action of one object coming forcibly into contact with another.*

The key here is that thoughts are real forces and have an impact on our daily lives. Thoughts typically begin with your beliefs. If you hold negative or difficult beliefs, they will negatively impact your actions and what you attract in this world. For example, if you believe it is difficult to make friends, then the impact is that it will be challenging for you to make friends. If you believe that you have to work hard to make a living, then the impact is that you will have to do hard work to make a living.

The impact of shifting your beliefs is tremendous. The subconscious mind, where our thoughts lie, is responsible for nearly 96% of all of our actions. Only 4 or 5% of our actions are dictated by our conscious mind. Think about that. The impact of your thoughts each and every day is where the success and flow or challenge and struggle of your life stems.

Many believe that your actions are a demonstration of the impact of your thoughts. I agree and when I look at my brother, I have seen how seemingly negative impacts were a constant force in his life. No wonder. He lived the majority of his life angry and feeling tremendous hatred for our father for leaving us after the war. However, the impact of his hatred and anger were manifested in all of these events dealing with impact.

When Jim was young, he was riding his bicycle to the store to pick up groceries for my mother. He was pedaling fast and trying to get there and back in record time. Not that mother had asked him to. But because he wanted to show her that he was able to perform and take over our father's role since dad was working out of town, as he was pedaling a car door opened right in front of him. He was thrown from the bike instantly and slung into the air. He was hurdled high above the car and his foot caught a telephone wire. He was left dangling upside down while the driver of the car jumped out to see what had happened. Luckily, he wasn't seriously injured in this accident. Just a few bruises and scrapes, but no broken bones.

The impact of something as simple as a car door was traumatic for my brother. When you have such anger and resentment that you carry around, it manifests in all sorts of ways. It is interesting to me that a "door" is what he was impacted with. In this situation, a door could have been showing him how to move into a state of happiness, less hatred and no resentment. Yet, the door's impact was only physical and did not have a mental impact on Jim's thoughts. In hindsight, I find it fascinating to look at the message behind the message.

Jim spent most of his childhood trying to compensate for my father not being there. Raised in a family with all girls and just one older brother, the brunt of the "father figure" fell on Jim. He was always trying to protect everyone and along the way was angry that his father was not there to take that role. Jim was at the playground and got into a terrible scuffle trying to protect our sister from a bully. He fought that bully viciously. It was as if Jim became an entirely different person. He was overcome with anger, resentment and hatred.

He beat that bully to a pulp. In fact, he took out two teachers and a nun principal because they were trying to break up the fight. He finally stopped when he looked down and the bully was knocked unconscious. Turns out the bully had a broken jaw and a broken arm. Jim was only bruised up a bit.

The impact of his hatred and negative thoughts was blinding to Jim. He couldn't even see what he was doing. He was just acting in a rage and on a mission to harm as many people as he could for hurting his sister. More importantly, I think it was all the pent up anger he had for our father leaving. The impact of these negative thoughts was extremely harmful to not only the other child, but also to the teachers and the principal.

As Jim was trying to help provide for our family, he was riding his bicycle making deliveries one winter day. There was an ice storm, it was November, and he technically had no business outside, especially on his bike. But he was determined. While he was pedaling down the street, a city bus lost control and ran right into Jim. Hit him head on. Jim tried to swerve, but it was too late. He was able to think quickly and grab hold of the grill with one hand the a windshield wiper with the other hand. His bike went zooming under the bus. Almost as if it were sucked into a vacuum. As the bus tried to come to a stop it kept swerving. With each jerking movement, Jim's hands kept slipping. As the bus finally stopped, Jim was flung onto the pavement and laid there on his back. He was shaken up, bruised and had scrape marks on him.

He was lucky that he was able to maintain his grip. Had he slipped while the bus was maneuvering its stop, he would have been sucked under the tires and likely crushed. The impact of something so simple as a windshield wiper or the grill of a bus can be tremendous. Even though it wouldn't seem so by looking at these items on the front of a bus, none of us would have that sense of appreciation. Jim certainly did and so did

Nine Lives Squared

I. The impact of something small can certainly be huge.

Jim was bringing home a brand new cupboard for his wife. As he parked the car, he and his friend got out leisurely planning to go in and have a glass of iced tea before they unloaded the awkward and heavy cabinet. The minute they climbed the stairs toward the front door, Jim's wife came running outside. She was in labor. He couldn't very well take her to the hospital with the cupboard in the car, there simply wasn't enough room. In fact, Jim and his friend had been hunched over in the front seat with the cabinet leaned over the front seat. They ran down the stairs and began to get the cupboard out of the back seat. It was a heavy piece of furniture. Jim's friend said he would take the top side so Jim was left pushing from the bottom as they made their way up the steep steps. By the time they were nearly at the top of the stairs at the first landing, his friend lost his grip. He couldn't hold any longer. As the cupboard slipped out of his hands, it came crashing down on Jim, forcing him down the entire flight of stairs and shoving him into his Pontiac car. As he hit the car, the cupboard bounced to the side and splintered into several pieces. Jim's back was wrenched and he was bruised and sore, but he couldn't even think about it because he had to get his wife to the hospital. When they arrived, the doctor told her it was a false alarm.

The impact of his fall was overcome by the thought of his wife going into labor. Jim didn't have time to even think about the pain that he was in until after he heard the doctor say it was a false alarm. At that point, he sighed deeply becuase he realized how much pain he was in. Our thoughts have complete control over our body and how we feel. If you don't believe that, just look at Jim and how he didn't even register pain until after the doctor's message.

Jim was always known for throwing hammers and tools around. I guess it was just his way of letting out his anger. This time it wasn't Jim throwing anything. His co-worker was beating the top of one ball

46

peen hammer with another one. He hit the top with such force that it was like hitting a large windshield. Only it wasn't glass that shattered in every direction, it was metal shards. Since Jim was next to his co-worker, he took the brunt of the impact. He had metal shards sticking out of him from his face all the way to his knees. They carefully loaded him up and drove him to the doctor where they removed all of the metal. Luckily he did not need stitches, only had deep cuts and wounds that required a lot of washing and rinsing to ensure they didn't become infected.

Jim swung his hammer in anger many days. Flung it through the air and aimed it at many different walls and targets. I don't believe that he ever thought of the impact one hammer hitting against another one could have. That day, he not only saw it, he felt it. That could have had a significant impact on his life and his actions had he been awakened to the universal law noting the impact of our thoughts. But he didn't.

Jim was working in a building when he stopped to take a rest. He had been going hard that day and decided he needed a break. He stopped and leaned against a wall. He was in what he thought was a "safe zone" because most of the finishing work had been done. While he was taking it easy, a fluorescent light fixture fell from the ceiling. The fixture hit his head and as he went sideways, the fluorescent bulb fell out of the fixture. As Jim hit the floor, the bulb's two pointed prongs hit Jim's temple on the left side of his face. They took him to the doctor and all he could do was shake his head. Had the bulb come out of the fixture from the ceiling, it would have had the force to pierce his temple and do serious damage.

Who would ever think about the impact and potential damage that could be caused by two simple prongs on a fluorescent light bulb? Two tiny prongs that are what cause the light to come on. Think about that. Two simple little prongs cast a vibrant light on a room, yet can have a deadly impact at just the "perfect angle."

Jim was on a scissor lift working at ceiling height in a warehouse with his co-worker. This was normal for Jim. He wasn't afraid of heights and was accustomed to dangling high in the air to get his job done. Today was a bit different. Just as he and his co-worker neared the ceiling, the scissor lift jammed. Jim jumped over the railing to start climbing down to the base. His co-worker immediately grabbed the remote control and started fidgeting with the wire. He hadn't noticed that Jim climbed down. He touched two wires together that sparked the motor to work. The scissor went down with force and luckily, Jim was almost to the base of the unit. It scraped Jim's forehead, tore his glasses off and scraped his nose as he dove off the side.

Another one of Jim's co-workers crossed the wrong wires when Jim was on a boom that was fully extended. The crossed wires caused the boom to drop instantly, leaving Jim in mid-air and crashing to the ground. He was bruised badly from the fall.

Getting your wires crossed normally doesn't have a tremendous impact. In this case, it certainly did. The impact of two wrong wires crossed can kill someone. Have you ever thought of it that way? Most of us pay little attention when people's wires get crossed with communication, but no matter what the wires are, they can have a detrimental impact.

One summer day, Jim decided to walk outside of the garage and get some fresh air. Well, he got more than that. His co-worker lowered a boom, not knowing that Jim was walking outside. It hit Jim square in the head, then hit his shoulder and arm. As Jim took a dive, it slammed next to him on the ground. He had a headache, dizziness and missed over 15 days of work because of his injuries, and the fact that they couldn't get his blood pressure regulated.

The impact of a boom is tremendous, but the lasting impact was on his blood pressure. I believe that he had high blood pressure before he ever got hit. With his anger issues, he probably needed blood pressure treatment sooner. The blessing of this impact, in my mind, was to treat the high blood pressure problem that had been brewing for some time.

Jim's teeth have suffered the brunt of several impacts. Here are two that come to mind. He was working on the body of a Chrysler car when the slip knot came undone and a 32' pick board came shooting into Jim's face. Before he could turn, he was nailed in the mouth. His face swelled up and he had to have his first crown.

The next time was when one of his co-workers lost his grip on a 16' plank that dropped through a small opening. That small opening slowed down the plank enough that when it hit Jim's face, it broke the tooth off at the gum line. If it had hit him with full force, it would have likely broken off several teeth or he would have caused severe damage to his jaw. Instead, he got yet another crown.

When we think of a crown it is typically associated with royalty or something positive. The impact for Jim was two crowns. I don't think that he saw them as regal, royalty or positive. For him, they were associated with pain and negativity. Yet, the lasting impact of something negative can be positive if you choose to interpret it that way.

There are weird things that happen in life. Jim has seemed to always attract the weird and quirky. He was sitting in his truck across the street catching up on paperwork. He was still on the job site, but thought he was safe in his truck. A lock drop pin fell 40' from the scaffolding above him. It bounced off the planks to the cement, bounced up and flew through the passenger window. The noise caused Jim to turn his head and as he did, his mouth was open as he wondered what had just happened. The pin flew in his mouth, cut his tongue and the roof of his mouth. Luckily, he did not require stitches.

I have never thought of a lock box pin as having an impact. Yet again, Jim proves the point that anything trivial and small can have a tremendous impact. Random things can happen causing an impact on one's life. This pin had an impact on Jim's mouth. Was he talking too much negativity and hatred? Was this a sign that he needed to speak more kindness and be gentler with his words? Not sure, but my belief is yes.

Jim was walking down a street when some drunken teens started harassing him and hit him with an empty beer bottle. Jim was using his walker at that time because he had just had heart surgery. This wasn't the first time that he was attacked when walking down the street.

Another time he was shoveling his neighbor's driveway when he had to dodge the snow plow. As he turned to run, he ran right into a telephone pole. He was thrown backwards and fell into the snow just as the snow plow went by. It buried him in a slushy mess. He had a large knot on his head from hitting the pole, but didn't suffer any significant injuries.

The impact that others can have on you can be significant. Something as simple as a beer bottle with the right amount of force can be debilitating. The impact of not paying attention for a moment can be costly and hazardous.

Another time we were scared was when Jim was riding his bicycle down the sidewalk and he passed out. No one even knows why, but he did. I wondered if it was his blood pressure that dropped or blood sugar that caused it. Needless to say, he ran into a telephone pole and was knocked off his bike into the street. Just as he hit the street an 18-wheel transport truck slammed on his brakes. The tires were squealing and smoke was coming out from underneath the truck. The truck stopped straddling Jim. The oil drain plug left a small indention on Jim's forehead, but other than that he just had bruises. Lucky that he was positioned perfectly for the truck to straddle him.

That would have had an incredible impact on Jim had the semi not been able to stop or if the truck had even been a foot to one side or the other. The driver made the right adjustment at the right time. Jim couldn't as he was still unconscious. I can't imagine coming to and seeing the undercarriage of a semi above me. The truck driver, new at driving a semi, was so mentally affected by running over a person that he never set foot in a semi truck again.

The impact each of us can have in this world is astounding. It takes positive energy, focused effort and being aligned with oneself. You can have an extraordinary impact if you choose to do so. To go from ordinary to extraordinary you must first look at the expectations you have set for yourself. Do you expect to have an ordinary impact in this world? Or have you set your expectations so you can have an extraordinary impact? If you want to make an extraordinary impact, then you will have an energetic vibration at a higher level. This elevated energy will attract both events and people to support you in being extraordinary.

Ordinary implies being stuck in a rut, and while in a rut you attract others in a rut. I believe Jim was in a rut for much of his life. He just didn't know any better. You know the phrase, "You don't know what you don't know." I believe that was the case for Jim.

He lived an ordinary life as a person with extraordinary abilities. He wasn't in tune and aligned with his internal harmony and vibrational energy level. When you are connected and in harmony with the potential impact you can have on this world, you will sense a significant difference in how you react to situations and also how other people react to you. You need to be aware of these reactions because they bear directly on your ability to fulfill your intention, and ultimately determine the impact you will have on this world.

To unleash your unlimited extraordinary potential, you need to unlock your imagination and recognize your internal power. Become synchronized with what you imagine possible and what you believe is possible. This level of synchronicity is deemed by many as the elite level. When you are in this space, you will know it.

You walk into a room and just with your presence you can have a positive impact on others. Not from an ego stand point, rather from a positive energy stand point. View all of your activities as functions of your imagination working, guiding, encouraging and even pushing you in the direction that you are intended. This is how you can have a maximum impact on this world.

Remember that even the smallest actions can have a tremendous impact on not only your life, but also others around you.

CHAPTER 5
Healing - Heal your mind heal your body

Healing - *To restore to health or soundness.*

Healing oneself is a myth to some and absolute to others. Dr. Simonton, a medical director of the Simonton Cancer Center in Pacific Palisades, CA, talks enthusiastically about the results he is seeing with his disease-ridden patients who are using visualization techniques. Many believe that the mind and the body are more intertwined than people once thought. It makes sense because the same pathways that carry cancer cells can be used to carry positive things.

Many refer to this as a "healing belief." It is how your mindset is programmed, or de-programmed in some cases, around healing. If you believe you will be healed, you have a far greater chance of being healed. The body is naturally designed to heal itself by releasing specific chemicals, triggering responses in the body and sending signals of distress to the injured area of the body. All aspects of our body are designed to create and foster a healing zone. The problem typically occurs when you start to eat unhealthy foods, increase your stress levels, waver in your positive beliefs and ultimately question the things that are happening to you, instead of taking responsibility for what you are causing.

A positive healing belief is required to support the body in promoting a healing environment. Jim suffered a significant number of injuries as you have read thus far. However, these pale in comparison to all of the medical issues he had dealt with. I know how much anger and hatred he carried. All of the pressure he must have felt trying to fill my father's shoes as a young man while protecting the family and ultimately feeling like he missed out on his childhood youth. Read about his medical issues and you will understand why I ask this question.

Jim had a history of suffering from nose bleeds. I'm not talking about a simple nose bleed that most of us occasionally get when the air gets dry or there is a change in barometric pressure. I'm talking about full-fledged nose bleeds. He could just pinch his nose and it would start bleeding. It wasn't just isolated to his nose either. His gums and ears would also bleed. The whites of his eyes would even turn blood red. He still cried clear tears, but it was weird to be around that much blood.

One evening we were sitting in the dining room after dinner and Jim got a nose bleed. It bled so bad we were all scared. It didn't just trickle, it was gushing. Mother gave him a quart milk bottle to lean his head over and before they could get it stopped, the bottle was full. They got it stopped and mother tucked him in bed. The next morning, Jim was awakened by a wet liquid running down his arm. Turns out he had a nose bleed that started in the wee hours of the morning. He hollered and by the time mother got into his room, the sheets, pillow and his pajamas were wringing wet with blood. She rushed into the kitchen and brought in another quart milk bottle for him. While Jim leaned over it, she wrapped him in a blanket and then loaded him in the car to rush him to the hospital. Concerned there was something significantly wrong, I remember mother asking my sister to grab the other jar of blood so she could show the doctor. She was a bit grossed out, but knew it was not the time to question my mother. When they got to the hospital, the doctor could not believe that two quarts of blood came out of my brother's nose in less than 24-hours. He had both jars tested, and proved that there was no additional liquid added and both jars matched Jim's blood type. Jim ended up getting three vitamin K shots to stop the bleeding. He also had to have his nose cauterized. The doctor told my mother that Jim had bled from both sinus cavities, above his eyes and from his nose.

What was Jim thinking at that moment when the blood started gushing? I have always wondered. I also wonder if he panicked at that moment. I am sure that I would have. But in all of the books I have read, remaining calm is the key. I also think he believed there was something terribly wrong with him. This would be a natural feeling for most people. As an adult that has studied extensively universal laws and positive healing energies, I now know the power of positive thoughts on the body's healing process. I wish that I could have shared that with Jim and my family then. As with everything, it all happens for a reason.

Jim not only had severe nose bleeds, he had allergies. We grew up in a time when allergy testing was not popular so the way people figured out what they were allergic to was through eating it and watching the symptoms arise. Turns out Jim was allergic to mint and didn't know it. It was a hot summer afternoon and Jim was hungry and thirsty. Mother didn't want him to ruin his appetite for supper so she gave him a handful of mints and told him he could drink a cola. He ate all of the mints and downed the cola. Obviously no one knew it, but Jim was allergic to mint and tannic acid, which is found in cola. Jim started hyperventilating. He hit the floor in the kitchen and went into a coma. Mother called the ambulance and when they arrived, Jim was struggling to breathe and he was having convulsions. They rushed him to the hospital where they injected him with a shot of something. We don't know to this day what it was. The doctor warned Jim never to eat mint or drink anything with tannic acid, especially in combination as he may not wake up the next time.

If your body is designed to heal itself, how can it have such violent reactions to certain foods and products? I have always wondered this as most people believe they can eat anything and drink anything. What causes an allergy? I think Jim's body was able to heal him and get him through this, but there was a point that Jim was to walk away with. As a child, I'm not sure he was capable of it, but now as an adult we have a far greater vision and light that can be shed on the body's healing mechanisms.

Jim had suffered a terrible back injury. I remember hearing stories about how he had suffered significant nerve damage. He was originally quadriplegic then as he went through therapy he progressed to paraplegic status. One day, he was strapped into his wheel chair and was going outside for fresh air. He started down the ramp, and at the bottom he missed the right turn to go outside. Instead, the wheel chair caught the corner of the railing, the chair flipped over the railing and he went flying into the pool. Strapped in, the chair sank to the bottom. He couldn't get himself out of the straps and panicked. Apparently, the nurses hit the panic button but none of them could leave their patients to dive in the water. One male nurse dove into the pool, unbuckled the strap, grabbed Jim and flew to the surface. Jim was limp and the nurse drug him to the side and proceeded to do CPR. He resuscitated Jim and everyone was quite shook up by the incident.

Panic set in for Jim when he hit the bottom of the pool. This is what so often happens to people. Their brains "shut down" for lack of a better description. The person goes into a state of paralysis and they are not able to even think, let alone function. They cannot process the steps necessary to even save their life. This state is heightened when a person is out of alignment and synchronicity with their mind and body. I know that Jim was worried about his recovery and was having a difficult time staying positive. I believe this contributed to his overall state of "paralysis" in the pool.

When Jim was in the hospital with his burned hands (from the blow torch experience), he had an IV in his arm feeding him with fluids. He had gotten extremely restless in the night and swung his arm behind his head. Sleeping, he didn't feel any pain or notice anything. Until the machine started beeping. He had kinked the IV which set off the buzzer. When the nurse came in, she examined Jim's arm and found that he had actually broken the needle off in his arm and it had traveled through his blood stream to his arm pit. She was able to locate it, but Jim had to be rushed into surgery to have it removed. He was in the hospital an additional week for recovery.

His body reacted to the lack of movement and with the jerking motion he caused even more damage. Jim spent most of his life flinging hammers around and other objects as he vented his anger. I believe this jerking motion was so natural for him that his body reacted instinctively to the way it had been trained and how he had programmed his brain. This instinctively programmed reaction caused tremendous pain and put him in the operating room. This just reinforces the power of the subconscious and reactive programming in the brain.

In an effort to heal several things at one time, Jim went in for open heart surgery and got a quadruple bypass, and while in there the doctors repaired a spot on his heart, strengthened a lung and then fixed a malfunctioning artery. Then they went back in and straightened his crooked sternum, repaired three herniated discs and broke three ribs to correct the fact that they had reattached incorrectly after some of his injuries.

All of these procedures were done in an effort to heal his body and provide relief from all of the pain that he was suffering from. He went under the knife to gain relief. I know that there were some issues that surgically needed to be repaired, yet I wonder how much of this could have been prevented with a healing body mindset.

In addition to sever nose bleeds, Jim had a problem of passing out for no reason at all. He could be walking, driving, riding his bicycle or any activity and simply pass out. He was examined by numerous doctors who all ran various tests, and not one of them could find a reason for this. His spells would last anywhere from a few minutes to 48-hours, and then in 2012 he was out for nearly a month. To this day, Jim is cautious about where he goes and how he gets there.

Isn't it ironic that the mind is the healing vehicle for our bodies, yet Jim is not able to "drive" himself to a healing state? Not yet that is. I am convinced that he will be able to heal himself of this issue when his mindset is shifted and when he chooses to reprogram his brain to heal his body.

Despite all of my stories, Jim has been pretty healthy his entire life. He has had more incidents and accidents than anything else. With Jim's heart problems, the doctor did prescribe nitroglycerin spray. It was weird. After each time he sprayed it in its nose, he would appear drunk and disoriented. I couldn't figure it out. I remember stopping by and thinking that he had been drinking, and when I questioned him he got upset and insisted that he hadn't. However, he certainly appeared drunk to me and I'm sure he would have failed a field sobriety test by a police officer. The next morning I asked him about it, and again he insisted that he was not drunk. I asked what he had eaten or done before I stopped by. He gave me a rundown of his food for the day and what he had to drink and then his nitro spray. I asked him if there was anything in it that he was allergic to. He went and got the package and couldn't see anything that he would have a potential allergic reaction to. The episodes continued. He asked his pharmacist and they insisted there was nothing more in the nitro than what was listed. He even went to the manufacturer. After enough research, Jim found that in the plant they use a small amount of mint oil to coat the bowl before mixing the ingredients. It was such a minute amount of mint, that they were not required to list it on the ingredients. We were again reminded of his allergy to mint.

Our bodies are extremely sensitive. Even the most miniscule amount of something that your body does not tolerate can have a detrimental impact. With a small adjustment in the mindset, what would the impact be on your body? Small changes can heal significant issues. When I looked up the meaning of mint, I found that herbalists believe mint promotes success, motivation, money and healing. Many believe that it is a cure-all that relaxes the nerves and stimulates the brain. Was Jim's own body preventing him from success, motivation, money and causing more stress by eliminating this natural herb? It will be interesting to see if Jim's tolerance of mint changes as he makes the conscious choice to shift his mind and re-wire his brain.

Jim currently lives with a brain aneurysm and as soon as he gets overworked or experiences a stress-induced headache, he must immediately rest. It is inoperable and he must be vigilant and maintain a heightened awareness to this. I believe his body is trying to heal him from the inside out. Yet, I also know that he must focus on re-wiring his brain and shifting his beliefs.

This I know is not easy. Our oldest brother passed away at age 56. Our father passed away when he was just 56 and his father and our 5 forefathers passed at 56, as well. The first heart attack Jim had was when he turned 54, and the doctors have claimed there is a degenerative heart valve that is genetic and only lasts for 56 years. I believe that he had been focusing so much energy and effort on the fact that he was to die at 56 that he had the heart attack. I also know that shifting the mindset will shift your entire world.

He made a decision after his stroke to force his body to heal itself, which it is doing. All of us have that same ability. Every person is different and there are different techniques that need to be embraced to make a permanent shift to heal.

Each of us must take responsibility for our own health, and take an active role in our health and the foods we eat. And if you become sick, don't just give in and admit defeat. As Dr. Albert Schweitzer always proclaims, "The real doctor is the doctor within."

CHAPTER 6
Gratitude – Be Grateful for Everything Everyday

The Law of Gratitude - *When people are grateful then they attract every good thing that life can bring to them. When people live in gratitude they are working in harmony, but it's not a free ride. Each person needs to work with the Law of Gratitude and practice daily the rituals that honor and truly magnify ones sense of gratefulness for all that is coming towards them and into them.*

When people become ungrateful they draw more drama, conflict and chaos into their life. Just as with the law of gravity, when you jump up you will come down. It's the same with gratitude and the law of attraction. It is a grateful heart that is the magnet for mental, spiritual and material riches. A thankful person will draw more blessings to himself.

When I reflect on Jim I think he has always been a nice person, he just often complained about his life, his surroundings and his situation. As I studied John Kehoe, I realized that Jim was living an ungrateful life, which caused him to constantly attract more to complain about. He was literally attracting the wounds that he was receiving.

In many respects, I believe the universe was sending Jim signals with all of the close calls and especially the wounds that he suffered. A signal to be grateful for his life being spared and a signal to be grateful for all that he had in life. I often wonder how many more signs Jim needed. Just look at the number of times he was wounded.

Jim was a child when he had five gallons of boiling water spilled down the entire right side of his body. His skin was almost instantly peeled from his body, it just rolled away. Disgusting as it may sound, he was just lucky that he did not get an infection. He had to play and sleep on the kitchen table in a homemade sterile pond for over two weeks while he got daily treatments to remove the old skin and sterilize the area.

Many would say that he did not deserve to be burned, and I completely agree. No one deserves to be in pain or be injured. However, a state of gratitude would have ensured that he lived life grateful for no infection, grateful for only a couple of small scars and grateful for my mother's care.

Jim has taken several falls that wounded him. In fact, when he was a teenager he was climbing a tree and fell out. He hit an axe and cut his leg to the bone. Many people would have lost their entire limb. Not Jim. He had minimal damage to the bone and just limped around for a week or so. Then a year later, he was climbing in the rafters of a cottage on a construction site and fell. He landed flat on his back. He hit the ground with such force that it popped his eye out of the socket and with all of the dust and debris stirred up, that settled behind his eye. He got an infection in his eye and it took him several weeks to recover because the doctor had to flush out the entire eye socket in order to re-set the eye ball. Another time, he was painting the peak of a two-story house and he fell off the ladder from nearly 200 feet. He landed in a lilac bush that just happened to have a large thorn bush growing in the middle of it. It took Jim nearly five hours before he could take a deep breath. He had several scrapes all over his body and numerous punctures from the thorns.

Then, Jim was knocked off the roof of a building. He had constructed all of the scaffolding from the ground to the roof, but found himself in a position where he needed to be on the roof. He leaned over the edge just as the crane worker lifted a bundle of planks, and in the process of spinning them 90 degrees it knocked Jim off the roof. He fell over 150 feet, and despite the number of twists, turns and collisions with planks on his way down, he managed to land face first on the cement. As the workers gathered him up to take him to the hospital, they realized that his leg was bleeding profusely. Turns out as he raced down, his leg caught an exterior bolt and tore his jeans leaving a large gash in his thigh. He amazingly only had one cement chip in his face and no broken bones. He was kept in the hospital overnight and was stiff and sore for several weeks.

Jim demonstrated the effectiveness of the law of gravity each time he fell as he didn't fly and he didn't rise. He hit the ground each time. Yet, each time he recovered he continued to live his life complaining about his world. I know that it stemmed from anger as a child, but the more he complained, the more obstacles and issues he attracted into his life.

As Jim used his brilliance, he found himself in yet another precarious predicament. He was working as a mechanic and the particular truck typically required five guys working together to crack the bolts loose. Since there were only two of them, Jim got the brilliant idea to tie a rope to the beams to crack the bolts. He secured the truck with a jack stand, then tied a rope to the pole and wrapped the other end around his arm. Then he hung onto the pole to start pulling. It was all working smoothly until the weld broke on the jack stand and the truck started to roll. Jim became the weak link that gave way. With the rope tied around his arm, it pulled five ribs from his sternum and cracked his sternum lengthwise. When the doctors pushed the ribs back into place they got tissue up underneath, which still bothers Jim to this day.

I know that Jim is a smart guy. He has always been able to figure out unique solutions. However, I've listened to his stories and have watched him suffer from significant wounds all of his life. He may be able to figure out the mechanics of a vehicle or how to build a house, but until recently he did not understand the importance of universal laws. In this situation, he was complaining that there were only two of them to do the job of five. Instead of going and getting five guys and being grateful for having friends that would help, his stubborn nature and ego got the best of him. And, it could have cost him his life and I am just grateful it didn't.

One thing I couldn't understand was Jim's issue with saws. One time he was using a table saw and the blade flew apart. As it danced down the table, the saw blade gained traction and it bounced up his left collar bone. As it grazed past his glasses it knocked them off and ran up his ear. When he went into the house to clean up, he found the saw blade embedded in the second step of the wooden porch, over seventy feet from the garage where he was working.

Next time, his co-worker was using a chop saw and unbeknownst to Jim, the co-worker was using a fourteen inch blade instead of a twelve inch blade. Jim was about twenty feet from the guy and as the blade disintegrated, metal pieces starting flying. Jim was hit in the left side of the face and in his hard hat, which slowed the flying blade enough that when it hit his wrist, it stopped short of cutting his artery.

As Jim was working in his garage, he passed out. Thank goodness he was wearing his safety glasses and face shield because as he fell, he hit a piece of angle iron that hit the chop saw blade. The blade broke apart and Jim got hit in the face. He laid on the garage floor unconscious for nearly ten minutes. He crawled to the house disoriented and had a blade scrape under his cheek, eyebrow, forehead and also had pieces of fiber disk stuck under his skin in several places. He went to the hospital several times over the next thirty days as pieces of material and debris continued to come to the surface of his skin. The family was certainly glad that he didn't have more injuries. However, his daughter was not thrilled when he walked her down the aisle three weeks after the accident with scrapes and scabs all over his face. I can definitely understand why Jim always said he didn't have bad luck, he had good luck because he is still alive and still doing a lot of the things he wants to do.

Why did Jim have so many close calls with saw blades? I can't answer that question, but I do know that the teeth of reality bite hard when you are not following the universal laws. Jim just didn't heed to those close calls and I believe that's why he continued to have close encounters. He certainly did not once question the why behind it. Just continued to say he was lucky.

Jim also had several other close encounters while on the job site. One day one of his co-workers dropped two steel plates into the hole where Jim was working. Luckily the first plate hit the dirt and stopped but the second plate hit the first and then slid and bounced hitting Jim directly in the face. It drove a piece of his left cheek bone into the eye socket just behind the eye. The bone piece was small, about five sixteenths inches in diameter and was nearly three quarters of an inch in length. Jim was taken to the hospital where they removed the bone, fixed the eye socket and as they were working on that, the doctor noticed there was a problem with the lens of Jim's eye. They fixed that and amazingly, Jim's eye glass prescription changed significantly.

On another job site, Jim was involved in tearing down the temporary casino site and a co-worker on the fifth floor hit a window to let in a breeze as he was hot. What the guy didn't realize is that Jim was directly below working on the second floor holding onto a window sill when a large piece of glass came rushing at him. The pointed end of the glass hit Jim on the arm, pierced the skin and hit with such force that it split his arm bone. It could have actually cut off his arm, but it didn't because it hit the bone. He was rushed to the hospital where they removed all of the glass and he had to wear an open cast so his arm could be treated for the next four days. Once they completed treatment of the bone, they sewed the wound shut and put on a regular cast. Jim had to wear that for over six weeks, then had to go into therapy to regain motion and strength.

Someone trying to gain relief for himself put my brother in significant danger. Jim's injuries could have been significantly worse. I look at the circumstances of why and how he was in that particular place at that particular moment. I hear of people who have close calls all of the time, and they are typically people that are living a world of gratitude.

I remember stories of this incident vividly because Jim was about 17, and he was working at the time and tossing glass into a bin. Someone had spilled something, maybe oil, just in front of the bin and Jim slipped and went flying head first into this large bin of broken glass. He had scrapes all over his body and his right wrist was severed in the artery. Luckily, he only had puncture marks on his neck, where his main artery is. He had over twenty stitches on his right arm alone, was in the hospital over a week and then out of work for two more weeks at home recovering. When he did go back to work, his boss had called the police to investigate because they thought Jim had tried to commit suicide.

I believe that Jim has lived his life out of alignment. He is just not aware of the power of gratitude and the impact it can have on life. And not only for his life, but others as well. It starts by living every moment of every day in gratitude. Each of us should be truly grateful for every incident, event and conversation in our day.

I start my day and end my day writing in a gratitude journal. I note the incidents that stood out and write why I am grateful for them. What I have seen is that through reflection I can always find something to be grateful for, even with seemingly difficult situations or incidents. Since I have started this, I am amazed at what has come into my life. I have had experiences, people and incidents that are truly a blessing for me. Even Jim has noticed a lot of what has been going on. I continue to share with him the process and steps that I am taking, all with a grateful spirit as I am truly grateful for who he is and all that he has experienced.

Chapter 7
Coincidence – The Universe's Way of Staying Anonymous

Synchronicity - *the simultaneous occurrence of events that appear significantly related but have no discernible causal connection.*

Coincidence – *a remarkable concurrence of events or circumstances without apparent causal connection, correspondence in nature or in time of occurrence.*

Many believe there is no such thing as coincidence. Yet when you look at what happened to my brother over the years in the following stories, you may wonder. I believe there was a greater, deeper reasoning behind each of the events.

Synchronicity is the synchronized occurrence or coincidence of events in life that have special meaning. Synchronicity arises from a chain of causality that originates outside the physical reality. You cannot see where the chain begins, where the original cause resides so the phenomenon is considered coincidental. However, synchronicities are whole packets of cause and effect spanning past, present, and future from an alternate timeline that are instantly inserted into the original timeline as a result of intention.

Synchronicity happens to everyone but the person far best qualified to comprehend them is the one who is experiencing the incidents. I believe synchronicities are personal gifts from a great, caring intelligence responsible for the destiny of the universe. The full appreciation of synchronicity is nothing less than our personal connection with the higher intelligence of the universe. Synchronicities can be seen as little miracles through which an unseen and non-forceful consciousness manifests itself into our lives.

It is the observer that shapes reality and gives it meaning through intent. I believe you should accept even the most obvious coincidence as important guidance.

Chance, coincidence or, in the word of Carl Gustav Jung, "synchronicity," defined as "the simultaneous occurrence of two unrelated or causal but meaningful events," definitely presents a serious challenge to the most fundamental assumptions or principles of science regarding the nature of reality.

Newton believes we live in an orderly universe, one that is governed by predictable and immutable laws of physics, such as, "For every effect, there must be a corresponding cause," or his famous Third Law of Motion: "For every action, there must be an equal and opposite reaction." One physicist was quoted as saying, "God does not play dice with the universe."

What is baffling and often leaves scientists scratching their heads are the numerous occurrences of coincidences which cannot be logically explained by any accepted principles of mechanistic Western science.

Look at some of the things that happened to Jim and there is certainly no mechanistic Western science that could explain these occurrences and sequences of events.

It was 1954 and Jim was sitting outside on a rock in a ditch. It was late in the afternoon and he was simply taking a break from a day of hard work. He finished drinking his can of soda, got up and started walking to his truck to head home. As he opened his truck door, he heard tires squealing and as he looked over his shoulder, he saw a car swerve and then careen into the ditch. The car landed on the rock that Jim had just been sitting on. Jim rushed over and as he saw the drunk driver stagger out of the car, he paused to reflect on the fact it was a close call for him. When he got to work the next day, Jim kept saying what a close call it was on his life. Merely seconds separated him from death or serious injury. The chain of events could not be explained and the timing is perplexing to our family even today.

In 1960 Jim and our mother were sitting on the couch talking about the day. Simple, relaxed conversation in the living room of our apartment that was above the Metropolitan Department store. As we talked, mother asked if Jim was hungry. Of course he was, it seemed that Jim always had an endless pit for a stomach! Mother suggested that they go to the local diner for a burger and fries. They walked out of the apartment, left the building and within ten-minutes, the building exploded. Thank goodness it was evening and the store was not filled with customers. And, thank goodness mother decided to go out to eat or they would have been sitting in the living room.

In 1974 Jim was working for a company that had underground oil tanks. He was tasked with handling welding repairs on the tanks. One day he lit his torch and began repairs on a 1,000 pound oil tank that sparked. Jim jumped and ran all in one motion. He was out the door and landed in a nearby ditch filled with mud. He sunk to his waist as the explosion hit. Unbeknownst to Jim, on the previous day an apprentice had accidentally dumped sugared gas into the underground oil tank. That's what ignited the tank and caused the explosion. Jim was just thankful that he saw the spark first as he barely made it to the mud before the explosion.

In 1978, Jim and his buddies were building a septic tank truck (pumper as they are commonly called). As they were working on it, the methane gas ignited and Jim was caught off guard. Jim and his co-workers were thrown through the steel door with the pressure of the explosion. Luckily, the pressure catapulted them out the door and away from the fire. None of them were injured other than bruises and scrapes.

That same year, Jim went in for carpel tunnel surgery on his right hand. They gave him a local anesthetic, so Jim was still conscious as the nurse started to prep his left hand. The doctor walked in and started to grab the surgical tools to cut open his left hand when he screamed, "It's my right hand, not my left hand." The surgical team jumped in shock. Jim was just thankful that he was conscious enough to alert them, otherwise he would have had a "bonus" surgery on his left hand.

In 1979, Jim and his co-workers were working in the crusher conveyer belt at the salt mine in LaSalle. As they were diligently doing their job, someone in the control room didn't realize that these guys were on the job and started the crusher. As they heard the hum of the crusher begin to roar, Jim and the guys quickly realized what was happening. They frantically took their tools and began to beat the machine, all while they screamed at the top of their lungs. However, their screams would never be heard over the roar of the machine. They beat frantically until they finally broke a piece of the equipment and disabled the machine. They narrowly escaped being crushed.

In 1983, Jim was on a job site and stepped over to his van to get some tools. He climbed into the driver's seat to lean over and open the toolbox in the passenger seat. He grabbed the tool and as he sat in the driver's seat, he hear this loud swooshing noise. He looked out the windshield just in time to see a 38' steel beam blast through the windshield. It came through on the passenger side and catapulted his toolbox through the van and out the back door. He sat shaking as he realized how close he came to being crushed by the beam.

Jim was driving his truck through town on his way to work when he was stopped by a red light. As he sat waiting for it to turn green, he was thinking about all the things he needed to do that day. As he looked up to see if the light had changed, he simply saw a bright yellow flash as the steel stoplight fixture came crashing through his windshield. He leaned toward the steering wheel covering his head. As he came up, he looked over in horror and saw the 3-foot stop light dangling in the passenger seat. His windshield was completely shattered and sparks were flying everywhere. Luckily, it had snapped the cable so there was no live electricity flowing.

In 1991, Jim had headed to the tire store to purchase new tires. He had spoken to his pals there, had his tire order completed, had just paid and was on his way out the front door. He saw a woman with a stroller approaching the store, so he paused to hold the door open for her. As she passed by, he turned and watched to make sure she and her child were safely in the store. Just as he turned and started walking toward the parking lot, a crane from across the street tipped over and the boom came crashing down crushing the front entrance of the tire store. He heard nothing until the swooshing of the boom past him. He hit the pavement and was covered in pieces of asphalt as the boom scrapped through the front entrance throwing debris in all directions. The boom stopped about 6-feet from where Jim had been standing helping the woman and child. Luckily, the woman and child were safely in the store and were not injured, and neither was Jim.

Jim was working in a sewage treatment plant where the company had large fans running all day to disperse the methane fumes. All the workers were busy doing their job, including Jim. All of a sudden the fans shut down and a voice came over the speakers indicating that they would be shut down for approximately 25-minutes for maintenance. No one in the plant thought anything about it because everyone was equipped with methane gas meters, as was the building.

In fact, if methane ever hit dangerous levels, it would always trigger an annoyingly loud alarm. Except that day. Someone caused a spark which ignited an explosion that sent a ball of flames through the plant, blowing hard hats off all the workers as it whizzed by them. Jim and his co-workers had no forewarning of this explosion that literally blew the roof off. Luckily, Jim and his co-workers were in the structural steel area so they were safe. After the explosion, they were all standing outside talking about how random the incident was and how strange it was that no methane gas meter was triggered. Every single meter in the building read normal, even though there was clearly an excess of gas that triggered the explosion.

In 2004, Jim was working for a company that was stringing pipe. He was tasked with handing pipe up the line to the workers above him. He was only a couple of weeks from having bypass surgery for his heart condition so the doctors had ordered him on light-duty with no stress. His job placed him in a chair to sit all day and simply hand piping sections up to the workers above him. Jim was doing his job and moving a lot of pipe, handing up bundle after bundle. Until all of a sudden a pipe came shooting down at him. Before he could realize what was happening, the pipe went completely through the chair he was sitting in. It went right between his legs, missing all the "important" body parts. He sat there in shock looking at the steel pipe that was standing in front of him between his legs. He had no injuries and no one on the job site could believe how lucky he was.

As I mentioned earlier in this chapter, synchronicity defined as the synchronized occurrence or coincidence of events in life that have special meaning. I believe that each of the incidents in Jim's life have special meaning, whether he knows it or not.

When I read about all of the seemingly strange incidents that I know were not coincidental, I look for the special meaning. Perhaps there is just as much meaning for others who are around Jim, as there is meaning for Jim himself.

When you hear something or see something happening to someone else, pause and be present. We have all heard that phrase, "You have to be present to be present." As you ground yourself, pause for a moment and get fully present into the situation. Experience the emotions and connect. Connect with the incident, the people, the feelings and all aspects of the situation that make it real. Digest this and be present on how you feel about it.

Then you can look for the blessings or lessons that apply to you. Even though the chain of synchronicity happened to someone else, you are present to it and are actually part of the chain. It will affect your next moves, your thoughts and your feelings, and this is how the chain continues. You are impacted, so find the blessings and be present to the gifts you have been given with the experience.

Chapter 8
Be One with Nature

According to Buddhism, everything changes in nature and nothing remains static. The world is so because it is dynamic and kinetic, constantly in a process of undergoing change.

It is thought that we are all one with nature since everything is pure energy. In nature, there are no static and stable things, there are only ever-changing, ever-moving processes. Rain is a great illustration of this. Rain typically is referred to as a "thing", yet is it nothing but the process of drops of water falling from the skies. It is in motion and not static because it takes the clouds to create then release it.

Even when you look at a tree, it is not static. That's why we are all one with nature. We are constantly in motion, evolving to higher levels within our own mind and performance. In essence, the physical environment of any given area conditions the growth and development of the biological components (i.e. nature) and this in turn influences the thought pattern of people that interact with nature.

Universal laws demonstrate that man and nature are bound together in a reciprocal causal relationship with changes in one necessarily bringing about changes in the other. In the modern world, man often alienates himself from nature. Jim has always enjoyed being in nature, but I can't say that he is at "one" with nature. Look at these incidents and you will understand why I make this bold statement.

It was 1982 and Jim found himself in yet another predicament. He was cutting trees with co-workers when the unthinkable happened. Jim had shimmied up the tree with the chain saw. He was cutting branches in order to minimize the falling impact of the tree, as it was a big one. The guys on the ground had ropes tied around the branches in order to catch them as Jim cut through each. However, one proved to be too much for the guys on the ground. Jim saw this massive branch coming towards him like a swinging pendulum. He threw the chain saw in one direction and jumped in the other direction. He fell 100 feet and landed flat on his back. He barely missed being taken out by the massive branch.

In 1999, Jim was cutting trees and was harnessed to the trunk of this massive old oak tree. He had seen his first challenge, which was a large branch about 80 feet off the ground. He cut the smaller branches on his way to the "big one." He shimmied up the tree trunk to the massive branch, started to cut it and felt comfortable as everything was going as planned. As he cut through the branch, it broke and dropped to the ground, causing a shift in weight that in turn caused the tree trunk to pull out of the ground. As it did, the force flung Jim around the tree like a tether ball and his chain saw went flying in the air. It cleared the roof tops of two houses and landed on the ground still running. Jim was beaten and bruised from hitting the tree trunk so many times as his harness kept knocking him into the trunk like a slingshot. His co-workers came running to his rescue, and he was only bruised. The only thing they all could conclude was that the trunk was actually rotten and the shift of the weight of the heavy branch caused the tree to shift and lift out of the ground.

Jim was never deterred by all of the things that had happened to him. It was 2001 and he was cutting trees near his home. It was a late fall day and the frost was heavy on the ground and the air was brisk. For Jim, it was an ideal day to be cutting wood. He climbed up the trunk of a tree and started cutting smaller branches with his chain saw. That was always his mode of action. Get the small stuff out of the way before moving onto larger branches. As he continued to climb the tree, he spotted his first challenge. It was a large branch but nothing that he hadn't seen or cut before. He got the chain saw positioned and began to cut. Jim had gotten lax that day. He hadn't harnessed himself to the trunk. He believed the tree was small enough he could do it without the safety harness. Not the case. He was about 80 feet up the tree working on this branch when it snapped. It caught the chain saw and yanked Jim's arm, which pulled Jim right out of the tree. He fell, with the branch, over 80 feet and landed on his side on an old Indian style bridge. He was stunned and dazed and trying to regain his thoughts when the old rickety bridge boards gave way and he plummeted another 30 feet into the icy water. Luckily, he had two buddies cutting wood with him that day who heard his loud scream when he fell out of the tree. By the time they got to the river, Jim was gasping for air and flailing in the water. They took their ropes off themselves and threw him a line and pulled him to safety. Luckily, Jim only suffered minor bruises and slight hypothermia from the bitter cold water.

Jim was in the woods just behind my house in 2009. He wanted to ride the ATV and buzz around while the rest of us wanted to go into town. We left Jim in the woods alone. We didn't think anything about it since he wasn't going to be cutting trees with a chainsaw or doing anything else potentially dangerous. We should have known better. Jim was riding the ATV and slowed for a bump in the ground. At that moment, a large branch fell from a tree. It knocked Jim off the ATV and pinned him against the ATV. He was dazed and confused. He had been in the hospital the week prior with a brain aneurism and the doctors had told him specifically to take it easy. Jim thought riding an ATV was taking it easy! He regained enough sense to realize that he was in a very bad position. His leg was going numb and starting to turn purple, and he didn't have the strength to lift or roll the branch off of himself. He finally mustered enough strength to lift the branch enough to get circulation to his leg. He kept doing this off and on for nearly 2 hours until the family returned home and got nervous that Jim wasn't there. Knowing his history, we all knew something was wrong and we set out on the other ATVs looking for him. As I pulled up to him, he was still trying to lift the branch so he could get some circulation. I yelled for the other family members to come and assist because I certainly couldn't move the branch by myself. Luckily, they heard me and came quickly. Jim is lucky that he was able to keep himself calm because the doctors said he could have easily ruptured his brain aneurism with the strain and stress of the traumatic situation. He only had bruises and cuts from the branch. He was kept in the hospital overnight for observation and then released.

Where we lived was often referred to as tornado alley. If a tornado was possible, it was going to form and hit in this alley. In 2006, there were two tornados that plowed through this area. After the first one, Jim was out back assessing the damage. He noticed a willow branch twisted and while he was standing there trying to determine if it needed to be cut down or just left alone, he was struck on the head by a falling branch from another tree. It knocked him to the ground and he fell flat. He laid there sprawled out and semi-conscious. He had a terrible headache and was stunned and dazed, trying to figure out what happened. My sister in-law saw it happen from inside the house and went running out to assist him. As she got there, he was regaining his senses and able to speak slowly. He gathered himself and began to get up slowly. He had a large bruise on his head and a sprain in his neck from where the branch hit him.

It wasn't three months later that yet another tornado went through.

Jim and his buddy Larry were outside cleaning up debris. Larry had brought his chain saw and was cutting branches from trees while Jim was gathering the debris and putting it in piles. Jim was working diligently when Larry hollered, "Watch out!" Jim turned to see this large branch rolling towards him. He couldn't outrun it because he was still limping from a previous accident, so he tripped and fell to the ground. The branch stream rolled over him. The log hit his head and scraped across his ear and the side of his face. He suffered several scrapes and bruises, but was not injured seriously.

It was the fall of 1989 and Jim was determined to clean out the dead debris in the trees in his back yard. He did this every other year and this was the year. He always liked to do it "Daniel Boone" style, with a hatchet and his hands. He climbed up the tree and was chopping away. Small branches were falling to the ground and Jim was happy as he felt he was one with nature at that point. Until he swung his hatchet and it got caught in a crevice of the tree, pulling it out of Jim's hand and jerking him out of the tree. As he started to fall, his head hit the blunt edge of the hatchet just above his hairline. He fell to the ground and landed on his back. He had a large gash across his forehead, and a big goose egg bump that was starting to turn purple. He was dazed and dizzy and he had to lie on the ground for quite a while before he could get up. No one was around to help him so he was lucky that he did not suffer more injuries.

Nature can lead and guide you if you are attuned to the messages and vibration. Being connected spiritually, as well as energetically, is critical for optimal performance. Many have said that Jim was not connected or "one with nature" because of all the incidents that occurred. I would agree in that he was active in nature, but not spiritually connected with nature.

That is a skill that takes concentrated effort and focused energy. You need to be present, open and aware. These are three skills that Jim was not familiar with in his life. I have spent the past several years studying, practicing, training and honing my mental skills to be more attuned, aware and present. It was that awareness that prompted me to write this book because I believe that people can learn from what Jim has experienced. Learn through his near-death incidents and understand how everything in our daily lives is a road sign. And I know that when you watch the road signs, the road of life will pave itself in front of you. Life is a journey and it is important to be one with nature.

CHAPTER 9
The Laws Explained

The Laws Explained.

Everything is energy and energy cannot be created or destroyed. It becomes the cause and effect of itself. Energy is in constant motion and is never at rest. It is forever moving from one form to another. Energy follows thought.

"There are no extra pieces in the universe. Everyone is here because he or she has a place to fill, and every piece must fit itself into the big jigsaw puzzle." Deepak Chopra

"Because of the Law of Attraction, each of you is like a powerful magnet, attracting more of the way that you feel at any point in time." Esther and Jerry Hicks

You are a Magnet.

With my brother Jim, many would say that he didn't deserve all that he has gone through in his life. However, I realize that each of us acts as a magnet. We each literally attract certain things, people, ideas and circumstance to us. It is the level at which we are each vibrating, and our energy field changes constantly, based on thoughts and feelings. For Jim, he was always in a negative mode. His thoughts were, "I'm sure I'm going to have an accident today. I may even die today." He expected it and thus attracted it.

However, I believe the universe was attempting to shake him up and awaken him to the fact that if he could pay attention, be positive and shift his thoughts, he could and would attract good and healthy things into his life. As many of us know, the universe acts as a mirror, sending back a reflection of the energy that each of us project. The stronger and more intense one's thoughts and emotions, the greater the magnetic pull becomes.

I realized this as I began studying and working diligently on my mind. After my husband passed away, I decided that I had a choice. I could wallow in pity or I could rise up and step into my own power. I didn't know what that power was, but I knew that I had been playing and living small for too many years. I had suffered from the verbal abuse long enough. I had listened and started to believe the controlling man that told me what I could do, where I could go, what I could eat, what I was doing that day and what time I had to be home. I resented him when he told me I was worthless, useless and stupid. I was tired of being controlled. If it hadn't been for Jim, growing up with him as my brother, I would have been much weaker than I actually was. It got to a point where fighting back and arguments were never-ending, it seemed.

I remember going to another seminar and it was to hear John Kehoe. I didn't know who he was, but I knew I could use some positive and good in my life. I sat in the audience like a child sitting in class the first day of school. What he was saying made so much sense to me. It resonated. It excited me and inspired me. I was motivated to do more and learn more. At that moment, I had a fleeting thought. Perhaps I was a widow at such a young age because the universe knew I had more inside of me. It was my time to shine, blossom and flourish.

I don't know what God has in mind or what the grand plan is, but I do know that day has changed the rest of my life. I was like a thirsty animal. I couldn't get enough. I studied morning and night, understanding the laws of the universe and I was feeling great. I was drunk with excitement and energized by what I was attracting in my life.

I had lived so many years with my husband where we spent very little money. We were always saving. We skipped eating out, we clipped coupons, we only shopped at the big sales and bought used clothing. I would go over a year without a haircut. According to my husband, it was his vision of how we were going to become millionaires. Well, he was right. We were almost millionaires by the time we were in our early forties. He saved and saved and we paid off houses and had new cars, but we didn't have a happy life. All we did was work, work, work. I would have much preferred a happy medium so we could have enjoyed more of life. And, then he passed away and never got to enjoy the money or experiences it could buy.

Jeff always said he was going to die young. I always told him that he would be around forever just to drive me nuts. Even to the last minute, I never thought he was going to die. My sister went into his room one day and told him (while he was in a coma) that Jane had finally found a great doctor that had some ideas to keep him going and hopefully keep him alive. Then Pam told him that if he didn't want to live like this, in a hospital or a wheel chair the rest of his life, he had best make up his mind. If he wanted to give up this is the weakest he will ever be, now was the time. The next morning when Jane came into his room, his eyes were open. I couldn't believe it. I called his Mom and Dad to come see him. Jeff would follow me with his eyes not moving his head or body. All day he followed everyone that came into the room. At 8 pm that night I had to go home, as 12 hours every day for 3 months was hard on me. I couldn't leave him alone much since I knew how claustrophobic he was and how he was stuck in a body not being able to get out and move around. That must have been devastating for him.

There was a very young nurse coming on duty and I had a feeling something wasn't quite right, but I was so exhausted. I tapped on the little TV that he had in his room and put on the hockey game. I told him to watch the game and that I would be back in the morning. I leaned down and kissed him and then left. The drive back to my brothers was interesting. I couldn't believe that his eyes were open all day. After I got to Jim's house and got ready for bed, I had a feeling again. Something wasn't right. I called the hospital and asked the young nurse if she had checked on him. She said she hadn't yet because of the shift change. She assured me that she would check on him and call me right back.

When she called me about five minutes later, she told me that he had passed away. I felt like I had been hit in the stomach and everything in my world changed at that very moment. I sat with all the money I needed to live. I was in a position of never having to work another day in my life, yet I started to wonder what more was out there. I felt unfulfilled and a bit lost. The more I dove into studying the universal laws, the more I saw of what could be, how I could be and what I could attract.

At that very moment, I realized that everything I had experienced was a result of my thoughts and how I had felt up to that point. I realized that going forward, I could attract the people, resources, ideas and circumstances to literally live the life of my dreams. But first, I had to think about what kind of life I wanted. I couldn't remember the last time I had a dream, let alone what the dream was about. I had never thought about what I ultimately wanted in life. I had just spent over 20 years in the motion of living each day in someone else's life.

As I studied, I realized that I had allowed my personal power to be stripped from me. I allowed my husband to take my power, my voice and stifle my belief in myself. I always felt like Jeff's wife and

TJ's mom, never felt like Jane or like I knew who Jane was. I had cowered to him and became a hard, raging bitch for all of those years. As I studied, I realized that I am more powerful than I ever thought and clearly than my husband ever thought. Or, perhaps he realized my personal power and potential and was threatened by it. Maybe that's why he was so relentless to strip it from me. Then again, maybe he molded me into someone that he knew would be able to take care of herself when he was gone. All the fights and arguments we had, I believe were because he had a plan in his life. He needed to make his wife, me, strong. I believe there was a plan for my life that would only start after his death. It took me years of trying to figure out who Jane King is to understand this and reconcile with this belief.

    I started to realize the power that was inside of me. I started to embrace it, love it, acknowledge it and appreciate it. I began to realize that I could do anything I set my mind to, literally. I started with a small exercise. I had always wanted to go on a vacation where I didn't have to worry about what the hotel cost, buying lunch meat and bread to fix meals in a motel room or wondering what the cool site-seeing attractions would cost.

    So I decided that I would plan a trip that I would want to take. I flew to Mexico by myself. I spent 7 days at a resort in the main Riviera. People were so great and when they saw that I was alone, they invited me to join their families on sightseeing adventures and other events. I jumped from a cliff, swung from a rope, dove nearly 20 feet into a large pool of water and went for walks on the beach at sunrise and sunset. I was lonely but I didn't let that stop me. I went out on one of the events the resort organized daily and I even went to a night club where there was a massive rave. I saw a person I had met at the resort and he kept watch over me while I partied until 3 am. I never had experienced anything like that in my life. I never thought anything like this was possible, and I never thought I could have so much fun.

Thoughts are things. I thought about what I wanted to do and I did it. Thoughts are real and measurable forms of energy. Every single thought a person has generates physiological change in the body. That's why it is critical to think and behave in a positive way that is in alignment and tuned in with what you ultimately want to be, do and experience in life. Act as if you already have that new car or are on the vacation of your dreams.

Thoughts come from the conscious mind, yet actually originate in the subconscious mind. In fact, most of the scientists and experts in the area of the mind have proven that the subconscious is in control. If the subconscious mind is playing negative tapes, they will overwrite the conscious mind. That's where my brother Jim was operating. He was constantly in a state of negativity. Even when he said he was going to think positive thoughts, he would still revert back to expecting the worst to happen to him every day. Jim was "normal" by many standards because he was so stubborn and could not let go of the negativity in his world or mind. He had developed an image of himself that he was accident-prone and likely to die at any moment in time. He bought into that belief and lived it every day.

I, on the other hand, had bought into the negativity of my life and my husband. I became so familiar with the negativity in my life, it became normal to me. My sister would point out how ridiculous it was, but I couldn't hear her. Well, I heard her but I didn't listen. It didn't resonate because I believed at my core the negative thoughts and actions I was living.

It wasn't until I went to that seminar that I started to release the negative mental programming and set out of my own comfort zone in order to make room for a more positive, healthy self-image and belief system. I was shifting my energy level and my vibration. I was allowing myself to more easily and effectively attract what I needed and how I needed it. And in a positive, empowering and loving way. And people started to take notice. My family wanted to know why I was so happy shortly after having lost my husband.

I assured them I was fine, but I don't think they believed me. I started to tell them what I was doing, but they didn't want to hear it, especially Jim. He assured me that he had always been accident-prone and would always continue to be. He just hoped he could continue to be lucky enough to escape death, but assured me one day he wouldn't be able to skirt it.

That was Jim's conscious mind speaking to me. He was rationalizing what I was telling him. He couldn't believe that energy could attract energy. Positive energy could attract positive outcomes. I didn't let it deter me. I was focused and on a mission. I wanted more of the good and amazing feelings that I was experiencing. It was like life was blossoming in front of me.

I read that joy is an internal guidance system. It is a personal internal feedback device. When you are feeling excited, happy and joyful, then chances are that you are on the right track and are living in alignment with your passion and purpose. However, if you are feeling depressed, sad or miserable then you are most likely out of alignment. For all of my marriage, I was unhappy. I was sad and always felt a bit depressed. Now, I feel alive and full of life. I know that I am aligned and living the life I am meant to live.

Not only does one receive internal feedback, but there is external feedback as well. Sometimes it can be subtle or not so subtle messages from people, incidents or actions of others. With Jim, it has happened all of his life and he has become somewhat complacent with it. Expecting things to always go wrong. For me, I just lived in a negative and caustic environment so what happened to me and around me seemed normal. Until my husband fell ill that is. I now view his passing as a significant wake up call (or sign) for me to listen and step into my greatness.

When I look back on my marriage, I realize that I lived in a world of negative emotions. I was always in fear of what my husband would say, think or do if he thought I wasn't following his guidelines. I felt resentment at times for the life I was living, but then I would rationalize it and tell myself that it was better than many others and justify it by looking at the bank account balance. The more negative emotions I experienced, the more negative energy and incidents I attracted.

Through the course of my studying, I realized that I needed to forgive my husband. I needed to release all my anger and resentment that I had and was not aware of. I knew that there were a host of feelings that I had repressed for too many years. The more I read, the more I realized in order for me to fully move forward, I would need to forgive him. Release that negative emotional energy in order to make way for the positive, free-flowing joyous energy that I was beginning to believe I deserved.

I had spent too many years allowing others to tell me how I should feel and I never realized that I had a choice. Even my mom used to say, "You made your bed, now you must lay in it." Each of us can chose how we feel, what we experience and how we view the world. When I was feeling badly, I now realize that it was a reflection of my judgments, beliefs, ideas and thoughts. I chose to perceive the situation I was in as one that I deserved. I believed it was the most that I deserved. Instead, what I realize now is that I was settling for less than I deserved and less than what I was intended to do in this world.

I hadn't made the conscious decision to choose happiness. I hadn't chosen optimism, and I certainly hadn't chosen to live in a constant state of gratitude and joy. I was living in a world of tolerance, acceptance and denial. I am now working on transitioning to a state of settling for nothing less than magnificence in my life. I realize that my emotions fuel my energy and my energy fuels my future.

"Dwell not on the past. Use it to illustrate a point, then leave it behind. Nothing really matters except what you do now in this instant of time. From this moment onwards you can be an entirely different person, filled with love and understanding, ready with an outstretched hand, uplifted and positive in every thought and deed." Eileen Caddy

I have made a conscious decision to focus on only the positive. I dismiss the negative and limit the amount of time that I spend with negative people. I have been working with Jim to enlighten him to the positive ways of the world and universal laws. However, he is not so quick to believe or embrace the concept.

However, I am learning more and more every day. I now know that the law of attraction doesn't filter the information that we provide. It doesn't decide what is better for us because we have free will and we decide where we want to focus our energy and our attention. No matter what we focus on, it will respond with more of it. That's why it is so critical to focus on what you want, not what you *don't want*. I realize that I spent most of my life focusing on what I didn't want and what I didn't like. Jim was the same. Always focusing on more of the negative, more accidents and more incidents.

"Once you replace negative thoughts with positive ones, you'll start having positive results." Willie Nelson

In my studies, I learned that every single word that is spoken or thought sends a signal to the universe. It creates a vibration that is either positive or negative. Now, I only focus on positive words. Words and thoughts of love and joy. Feelings of gratitude and gratefulness. Was it easy to transform into thinking this way every single day? No, it was not easy because I had been programmed for all of my life into thinking negatively, expecting the worst, accepting less and living a life of not honoring myself and my gifts.

I have worked for nearly four years day in and day out. I study at least an hour each day and I believe this has accelerated the results that I have experienced. Once I realized what I had missed, I was addicted to a positive and rich life. One filled with joy, happiness and gratitude. I love my life now. I am inspired to help others and to awaken those who still don't realize.

This includes Jim. I have been able to help him make baby steps, and he is now more positive and is having fewer accidents in his life.

Success Tools for Training your Mind

It is one thing to write a book that can help you become more aware of your mind and universal laws. However, I felt if I stopped there I would be doing a disservice to you. That's why I have given you tools in this section to help you. These tools are ones that I have used daily to help me along my journey of enlightenment and personal empowerment.

There are many tools to choose from, but I am sharing my favorites with you. Following are the journaling exercises that I do every single day. And yes, I mean every day. I made a commitment three years ago and have not missed one day since then. I actually look forward to my journaling time each day as it is a time of solitude where I can create an environment of love, light and peace while I write. I suggest you do the same.

Journaling
- Write 10 gratitude's every day. These are things that you are truly grateful for in your life.
- Write a list of those whom you want to say "Thank you" to every day.

- Write a list of what you want to visualize. Then read it morning and night. Focus on it and feel it at your core. Put as much emotion around the feelings as possible.
- Identify what your highest priority is for the next day.
- Free flow write what you think about most throughout the day.
- Jot down what you talk about most with people. Including those that are negative in your life and those that are positive.

What do you spend your money on and your time doing? Make a list and focus your mind on it. Make adjustments if it is not what you WANT to be spending your time and money doing. This should support your overall visualization of what you want in life.

Every day I remember that my unconscious mind is my second mind. It needs to be trained to think about what is important, not just wandering and thinking what it wants. It takes practice to train it and I personally spend half an hour a day doing this.

I have learned that you must be vigilant to the patterns you weave in your mind. You are the holder of these patterns and the key is in repeating them over and over and over. For example, I tell the universe, "If you put millions of dollars into my hands I will be an extraordinary custodian of it."

> *You are in control and you must be the change you want to see in the world.*

Worry only brings more of the things that you are worried about. So don't worry. Simply tell your subconscious mind what it is that you will be working on. This is what we are going to be thinking about. And be very clear.

When I am done journaling each day, I reach for my affirmations. Below are the ones that I have created for myself and I'm sharing them to guide you in finding your own. Or if mine resonate, use them. The choice is yours and the important thing is to create them. I have mine written on index cards. I created three sets so that I have one set I read each night, one set posted throughout my bathroom so I can reflect and read while I am getting ready for the day, and one set on my refrigerator so every time I begin to cook, I see them. Repetition is key. The more you see them, read them and absorb them, the more you align and move towards them.

Affirmations
- I have unlimited power at my disposal.
- I am worthy of uncovering my magnificence.
- My subconscious mind is my partner in success.
- I am a strong empowering woman.
- I am a confident disciplined person and I can achieve anything.
- Eating fresh wholesome foods makes me look and feel great.
- My book is bringing peace, hope and love to others.
- I am committed to being healthy and strong.
- The greater my success the greater my ability to help others.
- I nourish my body with natural whole foods that God has created.
- I am healthy and strong.
- I have a wonderful book that helps people to see that God is in thee.
- Visualize the life I want.
- I ask the universe if you put millions of dollars into my hands I will be an extraordinary custodian of it.
- I visualize millions of people purchasing my book and see it helping them find the right answers in their life.
- I visualize a great, loving and sharing relationship.
- My property is sold, all of my bills are paid and money is

coming in.
- I am tremendously successful.
- I enjoy and deserve abundance.
- My uniqueness is my greatest asset in making money.
- I vibrate with success and it attracts wealth to me.
- Opportunities are everywhere.
- I am always in the right place at the right time.

The mind is a sending and receiving station of thought. You are affecting your spouse and all of those around you by how you are thinking, and they are affecting you by how they are thinking. This is why I recommend that you pick good thoughts, good books, good TV shows and good music.

Thoughts are real forces. Every thought is energy, a substance, and has an effect on your life. Everything is energy so keep happy thoughts and happy people in your life. I suggest that you do a session to de-clutter your life of negative people. In many cases, this may involve limiting the time you spend with family because family, for many people, can be the most negative and toxic. There are many ways to do this, but the first is to create an awareness of those that are in your life that you are spending time with that are negative, and not supporting your positive lifestyle desire. Then, surround them in your mind with love and gratitude. Be grateful for the lessons you have learned from having negative people in your life. Bless them and release them. Then choose to spend time with those that mean more, support you more and are happy in life. You should create an environment of "positiveness" in order to propel yourself forward on your journey of transformation.

The thoughts that are emotionalized become magnetized and attract similar and like thoughts. When I am mad or upset it attracts more upsetting thoughts and events. That's why you need to be diligent about who you have in your life and who you surround yourself with. I only allow positive and caring people in my life, and because of this I continue to attract more positive, caring people.

You have the power to think any thought that you choose. If you are thinking negative thoughts then you are allowing them to be there. Realize they are there and then cut them off. Think of something else. You have the power to insert any thought into your mind. It doesn't even have to be real, they can be thoughts of success, personal power, confidence and abundance.

Outer World Influences

Don't let the things that happen in the outer world influence your inner world. When I was a child, I was chased home by a guy in a van. I was extremely frightened and it had an effect on my inner world. Until I started to do mind power work, I would be extremely afraid around strange men. As I completed exercises with my mind, I realized that I was allowing what happened in the outer world to impact my inner world. I give you permission to explore it and then search for ways that you can stop reacting to what happened in your outer world. Choose to no longer let it impact your inner world. It does not have to dominate your thoughts constantly. I made that shift and you can, too.

Remember…

These are things that you can do by yourself, for yourself and for others. You have a mind that you can control. Train it to think happy uplifting thoughts. Send love and happy thoughts to people that need it every day. You have this power inside you, everyone has, and we just never knew it was there. AND IT'S FREE…

You have the choice to live in a rut of hate, sadness, pettiness, selfishness and past disappointments that you dwell on all the time.

You may even have an addiction that you are always thinking of… the next drink, the next smoke or the next fix. Just know that you have the power to change those thoughts.

But you have to want them and have to be willing to work 30-minutes a day. It's only a half hour a day, yet you need to do it every single day. Success is in the repetition. It's just like a muscle in your body. You work it long enough it will become conditioned to react in certain situations. Your mind is the same.

Think of it as "Air Time." In order to live, you have to pump air into your body. If you were locked in a capsule, you would have to pump air in every single day to live. Start viewing your success like this and you can accomplish anything you desire. Look at it like you are living in a spaceship. If you stop pumping air in, you will die, which means you will go back to what and how you did things before. Keep the momentum by creating a routine and consistency.

Journaling

Date:_____

10 Daily Gratitudes
1. _____
2. _____
3. _____
4. _____
5. _____
6. _____
7. _____
8. _____
9. _____
10. _____

Who are you Thankful for Today?
_____
_____
_____
_____

Visualization List
_____
_____
_____
_____

Highest Priority

_____
_____
_____
_____

Journal Daily Thoughts

_____
_____
_____
_____

What did you spend your money on and your time focusing on today?

_____
_____
_____
_____

Affirmations

1. _____
2. _____
3. _____
4. _____
5. _____
6. _____
7. _____
8. _____
9. _____
10. _____

Date:_____

10 Daily Gratitudes
1. _____
2. _____
3. _____
4. _____
5. _____
6. _____
7. _____
8. _____
9. _____
10. _____

Who are you Thankful for Today?
_____
_____
_____
_____

Visualization List
_____
_____
_____
_____

Highest Priority

_____
_____
_____
_____

Journal Daily Thoughts

_____
_____
_____
_____

What did you spend your money on and your time focusing on today?

_____
_____
_____
_____

Affirmations

1. _____
2. _____
3. _____
4. _____
5. _____
6. _____
7. _____
8. _____
9. _____
10. _____

Date:_____

10 Daily Gratitudes
1. _____
2. _____
3. _____
4. _____
5. _____
6. _____
7. _____
8. _____
9. _____
10. _____

Who are you Thankful for Today?
_____
_____
_____
_____

Visualization List
_____
_____
_____
_____

Highest Priority

_____
_____
_____
_____

Journal Daily Thoughts

_____
_____
_____
_____

What did you spend your money on and your time focusing on today?

_____
_____
_____
_____

Affirmations

1. _____
2. _____
3. _____
4. _____
5. _____
6. _____
7. _____
8. _____
9. _____
10. _____

Date:_____

10 Daily Gratitudes
1. _____
2. _____
3. _____
4. _____
5. _____
6. _____
7. _____
8. _____
9. _____
10. _____

Who are you Thankful for Today?
_____
_____
_____
_____

Visualization List
_____
_____
_____
_____

Highest Priority

_____
_____
_____
_____

Journal Daily Thoughts

_____
_____
_____
_____

What did you spend your money on and your time focusing on today?

_____
_____
_____
_____

Affirmations

1. _____
2. _____
3. _____
4. _____
5. _____
6. _____
7. _____
8. _____
9. _____
10. _____

Date:_____

10 Daily Gratitudes
1. _____
2. _____
3. _____
4. _____
5. _____
6. _____
7. _____
8. _____
9. _____
10. _____

Who are you Thankful for Today?
_____
_____
_____
_____

Visualization List
_____
_____
_____
_____

Highest Priority

_____
_____
_____
_____

Journal Daily Thoughts

_____
_____
_____
_____

What did you spend your money on and your time focusing on today?

_____
_____
_____
_____

Affirmations

1. _____
2. _____
3. _____
4. _____
5. _____
6. _____
7. _____
8. _____
9. _____
10. _____

Date:_____

10 Daily Gratitudes
1. _____
2. _____
3. _____
4. _____
5. _____
6. _____
7. _____
8. _____
9. _____
10. _____

Who are you Thankful for Today?
_____
_____
_____
_____

Visualization List
_____
_____
_____
_____

Highest Priority

_____
_____
_____
_____

Journal Daily Thoughts

_____
_____
_____
_____

What did you spend your money on and your time focusing on today?

_____
_____
_____
_____

Affirmations

1. _____
2. _____
3. _____
4. _____
5. _____
6. _____
7. _____
8. _____
9. _____
10. _____

Date:_____

10 Daily Gratitudes
1. _____
2. _____
3. _____
4. _____
5. _____
6. _____
7. _____
8. _____
9. _____
10. _____

Who are you Thankful for Today?
_____
_____
_____
_____

Visualization List
_____
_____
_____
_____

Highest Priority

_____
_____
_____
_____

Journal Daily Thoughts

_____
_____
_____
_____

What did you spend your money on and your time focusing on today?

_____
_____
_____
_____

Affirmations

1. _____
2. _____
3. _____
4. _____
5. _____
6. _____
7. _____
8. _____
9. _____
10. _____

Date:_____

10 Daily Gratitudes
1. _____
2. _____
3. _____
4. _____
5. _____
6. _____
7. _____
8. _____
9. _____
10. _____

Who are you Thankful for Today?
_____
_____
_____
_____

Visualization List
_____
_____
_____
_____

Highest Priority

_____
_____
_____
_____

Journal Daily Thoughts

_____
_____
_____
_____

What did you spend your money on and your time focusing on today?

_____
_____
_____
_____

Affirmations

1. _____
2. _____
3. _____
4. _____
5. _____
6. _____
7. _____
8. _____
9. _____
10. _____

Date:_____

10 Daily Gratitudes
1. _____
2. _____
3. _____
4. _____
5. _____
6. _____
7. _____
8. _____
9. _____
10. _____

Who are you Thankful for Today?
_____
_____
_____
_____

Visualization List
_____
_____
_____
_____

Highest Priority

_____
_____
_____
_____

Journal Daily Thoughts

_____
_____
_____
_____

What did you spend your money on and your time focusing on today?

_____
_____
_____
_____

Affirmations

1. _____
2. _____
3. _____
4. _____
5. _____
6. _____
7. _____
8. _____
9. _____
10. _____

Date:_____

10 Daily Gratitudes
1. _____
2. _____
3. _____
4. _____
5. _____
6. _____
7. _____
8. _____
9. _____
10. _____

Who are you Thankful for Today?
_____
_____
_____
_____

Visualization List
_____
_____
_____
_____

Highest Priority

_____
_____
_____
_____

Journal Daily Thoughts

_____
_____
_____
_____

What did you spend your money on and your time focusing on today?

_____
_____
_____
_____

Affirmations

1. _____
2. _____
3. _____
4. _____
5. _____
6. _____
7. _____
8. _____
9. _____
10. _____

Date:_____

10 Daily Gratitudes
1. _____
2. _____
3. _____
4. _____
5. _____
6. _____
7. _____
8. _____
9. _____
10. _____

Who are you Thankful for Today?
_____
_____
_____
_____

Visualization List
_____
_____
_____
_____

Highest Priority

_____
_____
_____
_____

Journal Daily Thoughts

_____
_____
_____
_____

What did you spend your money on and your time focusing on today?

_____
_____
_____
_____

Affirmations

1. _____
2. _____
3. _____
4. _____
5. _____
6. _____
7. _____
8. _____
9. _____
10. _____

Date:_____

10 Daily Gratitudes
1. _____
2. _____
3. _____
4. _____
5. _____
6. _____
7. _____
8. _____
9. _____
10. _____

Who are you Thankful for Today?
_____
_____
_____
_____

Visualization List
_____
_____
_____
_____

Highest Priority

_____
_____
_____
_____

Journal Daily Thoughts

_____
_____
_____
_____

What did you spend your money on and your time focusing on today?

_____
_____
_____
_____

Affirmations

1. _____
2. _____
3. _____
4. _____
5. _____
6. _____
7. _____
8. _____
9. _____
10. _____

Date:_____

10 Daily Gratitudes
1. _____
2. _____
3. _____
4. _____
5. _____
6. _____
7. _____
8. _____
9. _____
10. _____

Who are you Thankful for Today?
_____
_____
_____
_____

Visualization List
_____
_____
_____
_____

Highest Priority

_____
_____
_____
_____

Journal Daily Thoughts

_____
_____
_____
_____

What did you spend your money on and your time focusing on today?

_____
_____
_____
_____

Affirmations

1. _____
2. _____
3. _____
4. _____
5. _____
6. _____
7. _____
8. _____
9. _____
10. _____

Date:_____

10 Daily Gratitudes

1. _____
2. _____
3. _____
4. _____
5. _____
6. _____
7. _____
8. _____
9. _____
10. _____

Who are you Thankful for Today?

_____
_____
_____
_____

Visualization List

_____
_____
_____
_____

Highest Priority

_____
_____
_____
_____

Journal Daily Thoughts

_____
_____
_____
_____

What did you spend your money on and your time focusing on today?

_____
_____
_____
_____

Affirmations

1. _____
2. _____
3. _____
4. _____
5. _____
6. _____
7. _____
8. _____
9. _____
10. _____

Date:_____

10 Daily Gratitudes
1. _____
2. _____
3. _____
4. _____
5. _____
6. _____
7. _____
8. _____
9. _____
10. _____

Who are you Thankful for Today?
_____
_____
_____
_____

Visualization List
_____
_____
_____
_____

Highest Priority

_____
_____
_____
_____

Journal Daily Thoughts

_____
_____
_____
_____

What did you spend your money on and your time focusing on today?

_____
_____
_____
_____

Affirmations

1. _____
2. _____
3. _____
4. _____
5. _____
6. _____
7. _____
8. _____
9. _____
10. _____

Date:_____

10 Daily Gratitudes
1. _____
2. _____
3. _____
4. _____
5. _____
6. _____
7. _____
8. _____
9. _____
10. _____

Who are you Thankful for Today?
_____
_____
_____
_____

Visualization List
_____
_____
_____
_____

Highest Priority

_____
_____
_____
_____

Journal Daily Thoughts

_____
_____
_____
_____

What did you spend your money on and your time focusing on today?

_____
_____
_____
_____

Affirmations

1. _____
2. _____
3. _____
4. _____
5. _____
6. _____
7. _____
8. _____
9. _____
10. _____

Date:_____

10 Daily Gratitudes

1. _____
2. _____
3. _____
4. _____
5. _____
6. _____
7. _____
8. _____
9. _____
10. _____

Who are you Thankful for Today?

_____
_____
_____
_____

Visualization List

_____
_____
_____
_____

Highest Priority

_____
_____
_____
_____

Journal Daily Thoughts

_____
_____
_____
_____

What did you spend your money on and your time focusing on today?

_____
_____
_____
_____

Affirmations

1. _____
2. _____
3. _____
4. _____
5. _____
6. _____
7. _____
8. _____
9. _____
10. _____

Date:_____

10 Daily Gratitudes
1. _____
2. _____
3. _____
4. _____
5. _____
6. _____
7. _____
8. _____
9. _____
10. _____

Who are you Thankful for Today?
_____
_____
_____
_____

Visualization List
_____
_____
_____
_____

Highest Priority

_____
_____
_____
_____

Journal Daily Thoughts

_____
_____
_____
_____

What did you spend your money on and your time focusing on today?

_____
_____
_____
_____

Affirmations

1. _____
2. _____
3. _____
4. _____
5. _____
6. _____
7. _____
8. _____
9. _____
10. _____

Date:_____

10 Daily Gratitudes

1. _____
2. _____
3. _____
4. _____
5. _____
6. _____
7. _____
8. _____
9. _____
10. _____

Who are you Thankful for Today?

_____
_____
_____
_____

Visualization List

_____
_____
_____
_____

Highest Priority

_____
_____
_____
_____

Journal Daily Thoughts

_____
_____
_____
_____

What did you spend your money on and your time focusing on today?

_____
_____
_____
_____

Affirmations

1. _____
2. _____
3. _____
4. _____
5. _____
6. _____
7. _____
8. _____
9. _____
10. _____

Date:_____

10 Daily Gratitudes
1. _____
2. _____
3. _____
4. _____
5. _____
6. _____
7. _____
8. _____
9. _____
10. _____

Who are you Thankful for Today?
_____
_____
_____
_____

Visualization List
_____
_____
_____
_____

Highest Priority

_____
_____
_____
_____

Journal Daily Thoughts

_____
_____
_____
_____

What did you spend your money on and your time focusing on today?

_____
_____
_____
_____

Affirmations

1. _____
2. _____
3. _____
4. _____
5. _____
6. _____
7. _____
8. _____
9. _____
10. _____

Date:_____

10 Daily Gratitudes
1. _____
2. _____
3. _____
4. _____
5. _____
6. _____
7. _____
8. _____
9. _____
10. _____

Who are you Thankful for Today?
_____
_____
_____
_____

Visualization List
_____
_____
_____
_____

Highest Priority

_____
_____
_____
_____

Journal Daily Thoughts

_____
_____
_____
_____

What did you spend your money on and your time focusing on today?

_____
_____
_____
_____

Affirmations

1. _____
2. _____
3. _____
4. _____
5. _____
6. _____
7. _____
8. _____
9. _____
10. _____

Date:_____

10 Daily Gratitudes
1. _____
2. _____
3. _____
4. _____
5. _____
6. _____
7. _____
8. _____
9. _____
10. _____

Who are you Thankful for Today?
_____
_____
_____
_____

Visualization List
_____
_____
_____
_____

Highest Priority
_____
_____
_____
_____

Journal Daily Thoughts
_____
_____
_____
_____

What did you spend your money on and your time focusing on today?
_____
_____
_____
_____

Affirmations

1. _____
2. _____
3. _____
4. _____
5. _____
6. _____
7. _____
8. _____
9. _____
10. _____

Date:_____

10 Daily Gratitudes
1. _____
2. _____
3. _____
4. _____
5. _____
6. _____
7. _____
8. _____
9. _____
10. _____

Who are you Thankful for Today?
_____
_____
_____
_____

Visualization List
_____
_____
_____
_____

Highest Priority

_____
_____
_____
_____

Journal Daily Thoughts

_____
_____
_____
_____

What did you spend your money on and your time focusing on today?

_____
_____
_____
_____

Affirmations

1. _____
2. _____
3. _____
4. _____
5. _____
6. _____
7. _____
8. _____
9. _____
10. _____

Date:_____

10 Daily Gratitudes
1. _____
2. _____
3. _____
4. _____
5. _____
6. _____
7. _____
8. _____
9. _____
10. _____

Who are you Thankful for Today?
_____
_____
_____
_____

Visualization List
_____
_____
_____
_____

Highest Priority

_____
_____
_____
_____

Journal Daily Thoughts

_____
_____
_____
_____

What did you spend your money on and your time focusing on today?

_____
_____
_____
_____

Affirmations

1. _____
2. _____
3. _____
4. _____
5. _____
6. _____
7. _____
8. _____
9. _____
10. _____

Date:_____

10 Daily Gratitudes
1. _____
2. _____
3. _____
4. _____
5. _____
6. _____
7. _____
8. _____
9. _____
10. _____

Who are you Thankful for Today?
_____
_____
_____
_____

Visualization List
_____
_____
_____
_____

Highest Priority

_____
_____
_____
_____

Journal Daily Thoughts

_____
_____
_____
_____

What did you spend your money on and your time focusing on today?

_____
_____
_____
_____

Affirmations

1. _____
2. _____
3. _____
4. _____
5. _____
6. _____
7. _____
8. _____
9. _____
10. _____

Date:_____

10 Daily Gratitudes
1. _____
2. _____
3. _____
4. _____
5. _____
6. _____
7. _____
8. _____
9. _____
10. _____

Who are you Thankful for Today?
_____
_____
_____
_____

Visualization List
_____
_____
_____
_____

Highest Priority

_____
_____
_____
_____

Journal Daily Thoughts

_____
_____
_____
_____

What did you spend your money on and your time focusing on today?

_____
_____
_____
_____

Affirmations

1. _____
2. _____
3. _____
4. _____
5. _____
6. _____
7. _____
8. _____
9. _____
10. _____

Date:_____

10 Daily Gratitudes
1. _____
2. _____
3. _____
4. _____
5. _____
6. _____
7. _____
8. _____
9. _____
10. _____

Who are you Thankful for Today?
_____
_____
_____
_____

Visualization List
_____
_____
_____
_____

Highest Priority

_____
_____
_____
_____

Journal Daily Thoughts

_____
_____
_____
_____

What did you spend your money on and your time focusing on today?

_____
_____
_____
_____

Affirmations

1. _____
2. _____
3. _____
4. _____
5. _____
6. _____
7. _____
8. _____
9. _____
10. _____

Date:_____

10 Daily Gratitudes
1. _____
2. _____
3. _____
4. _____
5. _____
6. _____
7. _____
8. _____
9. _____
10. _____

Who are you Thankful for Today?
_____
_____
_____
_____

Visualization List
_____
_____
_____
_____

Highest Priority

_____
_____
_____
_____

Journal Daily Thoughts

_____
_____
_____
_____

What did you spend your money on and your time focusing on today?

_____
_____
_____
_____

Affirmations

1. _____
2. _____
3. _____
4. _____
5. _____
6. _____
7. _____
8. _____
9. _____
10. _____

Date:_____

10 Daily Gratitudes

1. _____
2. _____
3. _____
4. _____
5. _____
6. _____
7. _____
8. _____
9. _____
10. _____

Who are you Thankful for Today?

_____
_____
_____
_____

Visualization List

_____
_____
_____
_____

Highest Priority

_____
_____
_____
_____

Journal Daily Thoughts

_____
_____
_____
_____

What did you spend your money on and your time focusing on today?

_____
_____
_____
_____

Affirmations

1. _____
2. _____
3. _____
4. _____
5. _____
6. _____
7. _____
8. _____
9. _____
10. _____

Date:_____

10 Daily Gratitudes
1. _____
2. _____
3. _____
4. _____
5. _____
6. _____
7. _____
8. _____
9. _____
10. _____

Who are you Thankful for Today?
_____
_____
_____
_____

Visualization List
_____
_____
_____
_____

Highest Priority

_____
_____
_____
_____

Journal Daily Thoughts

_____
_____
_____
_____

What did you spend your money on and your time focusing on today?

_____
_____
_____
_____

Affirmations

1. _____
2. _____
3. _____
4. _____
5. _____
6. _____
7. _____
8. _____
9. _____
10. _____

Date:_____

10 Daily Gratitudes
1. _____
2. _____
3. _____
4. _____
5. _____
6. _____
7. _____
8. _____
9. _____
10. _____

Who are you Thankful for Today?
_____
_____
_____
_____

Visualization List
_____
_____
_____
_____

Highest Priority

_____
_____
_____
_____

Journal Daily Thoughts

_____
_____
_____
_____

What did you spend your money on and your time focusing on today?

_____
_____
_____
_____

Affirmations

1. _____
2. _____
3. _____
4. _____
5. _____
6. _____
7. _____
8. _____
9. _____
10. _____

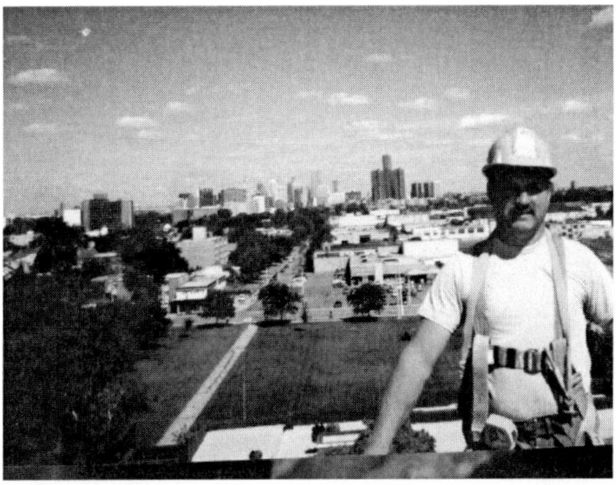

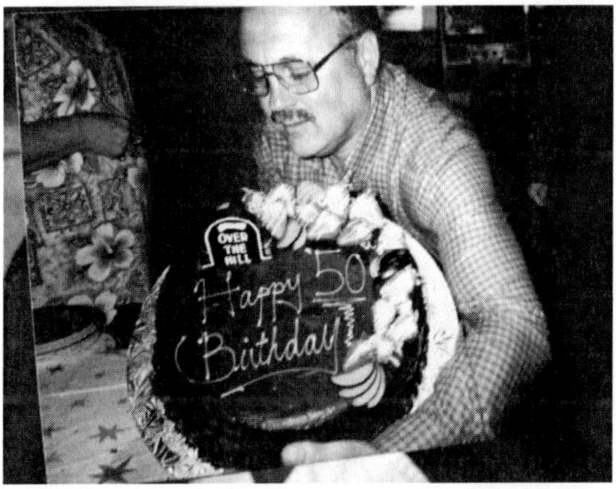
OVER THE HILL
Happy 50
Birthday

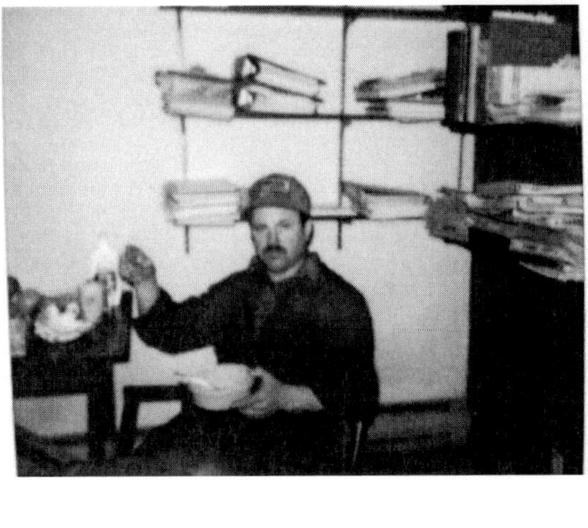

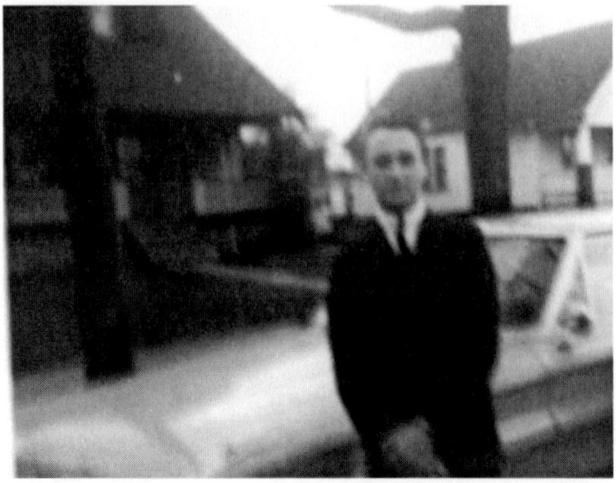

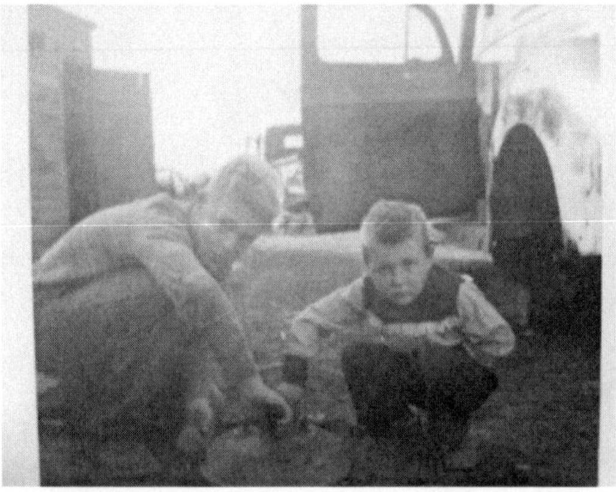

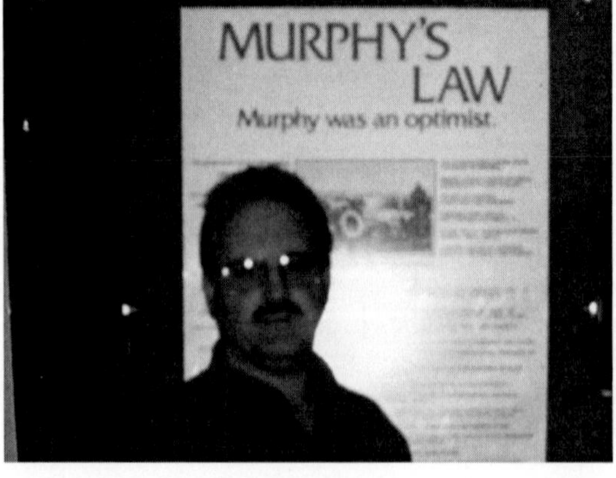
MURPHY'S
LAW
Murphy was an optimist.

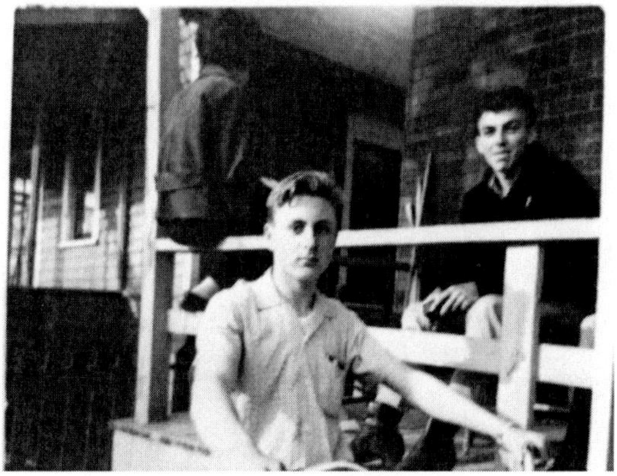

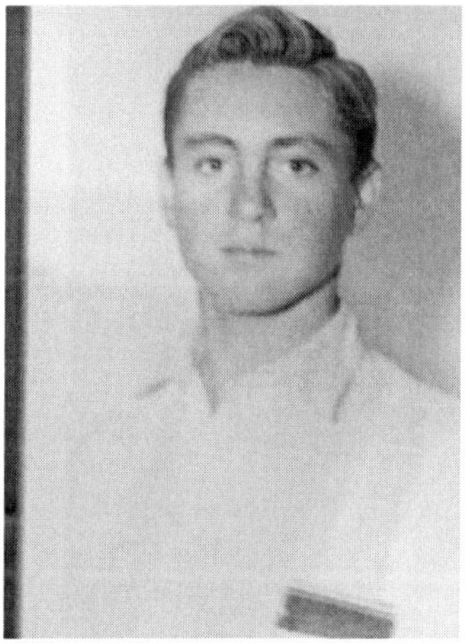

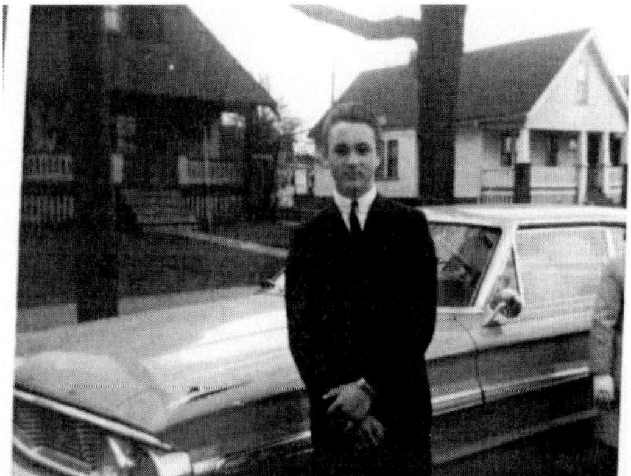